WEB-BASED NEURAL NETS: INTERACTIVE ARTIFICIAL NEURAL NETWORKS FOR THE INTERNET

WEB-BASED NEURAL NETS: INTERACTIVE ARTIFICIAL NEURAL NETWORKS FOR THE INTERNET

Introduction & Tricks

Marcelo Bosque

Translated by Angela Sabatini

iUniverse, Inc.

New York Lincoln Shanghai

WEB-BASED NEURAL NETS:
INTERACTIVE ARTIFICIAL NEURAL NETWORKS
FOR THE INTERNET
Introduction & Tricks

iUniverse, Inc.

For information address:
iUniverse, Inc.
2021 Pine Lake Road, Suite 100
Lincoln, NE 68512
www.iuniverse.com

Original Name: Redes Neuronales Interactivas para Internet (2004)

Translation from Spanish by: Angela Sabatini-Bartra—
Certified Translator (University of Buenos Aires)

Copyediting: iUniverse

ISBN: 0-595-31771-5

Printed in the United States of America

To Mary

There are many people that have helped me and given me their support and sympathy. Thanks to all of them. I particularly would like to thank Dr. José Seoane, former senior professor at the University of Buenos Aires, for his support, and Mrs. Angela Sabatini-Bartra, who translated this book into English. I hope that readers will be pleased with her work.

"An idea is just a new combination of old elements."

—James Webb Young

CONTENTS

List of Tables xv

Preface xvii

Glossary & Abbreviations xxi

Introduction 1

PART I
General Concepts about Neural Networks

Chapter 1 7
    What is a Neural Network? 7

PART II
Neural Networks: Usual architectures

Chapter 2 19
    What is an architecture? 19
    BPN: Backward Propagation Network 19
    BPN: Equations involved 22
    BPN: Forward & Back Propagation 25
    BPN—How does the N-Net learn?: Training & Executing the net 25
    BPN: Getting suitable weights 27
    Summary 28
    BPN: Setting the trend 29
    BPN training: Summary 30
    Activation and Output functions 31
    Choosing an Activation Function 31
    Usual Activation Functions 32

BPN: Mathematical Equations to make a 3-layer Back-Prop 35
BPN: Execution and training of the Neural Network 38
4L-BPN:Four-Layer Back Propagation Network 40
4L-BPN: Mathematical equations to make a 4-layer Back-prop 46
PHL: Networks with parallel hidden layers 49
SOMN: Self Organizing Map Networks...51
SAM: Self Associative Memory Networks (SAM) 56
Jump Connection Networks 63

Summary 64
Frequent Devices used to Capture Data 64
Forward & Back Propagation 67

Chapter 3 69
How to Input Data into the Neural Network 69
Digital images: Basic principles 69
Proper Formats for the Patterns 74
Working with Patterns Stored in Text Files 75
Working with Patterns Stored in Graphic Files 76
Converting the Image into an Input Pattern 80
Final step: Entering the Input Pattern in the Net 81

PART III
Design of a Web-based Neural Network

Chapter 4 87
What is a Web-based Neural Network? 87
Why we have to use them? 87
What do we do? Where do we start? 88
Designing a Web-based Neural Network.
First approach to the problem. 89
Point 1: Language of the Net 89
Point 2: Election of the Environment 90
Point 3: Hosting 91
Point 4: Choosing the Architecture 91
Point 5: Esthetic versus Speed 92
Point 6: Beware of Time-Consuming Java Scripts 92
Using Scripts to show the values online 93
Point 7: Creating the Site: Frames 93
Steps to Design a Web-based Neural Network 94

Chapter 5 97

  Building the Network: Databases, Tables,
  Environmental Variables, and Main Functions 97
  Databases: Defining where to store data *97*
  Data Structure *98*
  Permanent Storage Tables *98*
  Temporary Working Tables *100*
  Environmental Variables *100*
  Maximum Size of Patterns *100*
  Total Number of Patterns *101*
  Hidden Weight Layer Size *101*
  Current Pattern Number *101*
  Minimum Acceptable Error *102*
  Number of iterations before we End Training *102*
  Learning Speed *103*
  Main Functions *103*

Chapter 6 105

  Using the Net
  Sample Exercises 105
  Sample Exercise #1: Telling the Net to Recognize Shapes *106*
  Sample Exercise #2: Teaching Logic to the Net *111*
  Sample Exercise #3: Teaching the Net How to Recognize Numbers *115*
  Sample Exercise #4: Teaching the Net to Read *118*

Epilogue 123

  Source Code for a Sample Neural Network 123

Conclusions 125

Appendix A 127

Appendix B 131

About the Author 137

Bibliography 139

Index 145

LIST OF TABLES

Basic Background Symbols 2

Basic Foreground Symbols 3

Process of thoughts considering mind functions 11

Environment of a neuron 13

Artificial Equivalence between Biological and Artificial elements 16

Basic Scheme of a 3-layer BPN 20

3-Layer Back Propagation Network 21

Usual activation Functions 32

Execution of a Neural Network (Execution mode) 38

Neural Network Training System 39

Basic Scheme of a 4-Layer BPN 40

4-Layer Back Propagation Network 41

Basic Scheme of a network with parallel hidden layers 50

Basic Scheme of a Self Organizing Map Network 51

Self Organizing Map Network 52

Basic Scheme of a Self Associative Memory Network 58

Self Associative Memory Network 59

PREFACE

Mediocre minds feel terrified when they find themselves in front of the simple facts (of life).

—*Edward De Bono*

Many people feel that there are some subjects that ordinary people should not understand or attempt to learn. Certainly, there is a general preconception that neural networks, as a field of science, are too complicated for most people to comprehend. Thus, any attempt to simplify and facilitate understanding and learning in this field is met with sharp criticism.

Web Neural Networks was written primarily for students, amateur programmers, and others who want to know more about neural networks and how they can be used in conjunction with the Internet. My goal was to make this book as simple as possible. For example, few mathematical equations are included. In fact, if you are not particularly adept at math, you can skip the algorithms and still learn the basic principles of neural networks and the web.

Though I have written a summary explanation of the most popular types of nets, the book itself is focused on the backward propagation model, which is the most popular architecture for N-Nets. To see a Neural Network for the Internet, readers may access my web site, which includes the networking and load samples. Readers can also make load trials and download the source code to obtain the equations.

It is my hope that readers will find *Web Neural Networks* to be a worthwhile learning experience and as satisfying to read as it was for me to produce.

ACKNOWLEDGEMENTS

This book is dedicated to my students at U.B.A. and all the people who encouraged my work and gave me their support and empathy. Thank you very much indeed.

Marcelo Bosque

GLOSSARY & ABBREVIATIONS

3L-BPN: Three Layer Back-Propagation Network. See "Back-Propagation Network"

4L-BPN: Four-Layer Back-Propagation Network. See "Back-Propagation Network"

Activation Function: A computer function that modifies the input layer to calculate the hidden layers. It depends on the programmers' decision. The choice of an activation function is a mark, a craftsman work of the human programmer.

AI: Artificial Intelligence

ANN: Artificial Neural Network. See "Artificial Neural Network"

Artificial Neural Network: A form of computer software based in the architecture of the biological neural network of the human brain. It is especially useful in pattern recognition.

Backward Propagation Network (BPN): Back-Propagation Network

Back-Propagation Network: A sort of neural network. It generally has one input layer, one output layer, and one or more hidden layers. To train the net, the weights are propagated forward and backward, creating a recursive feedback training.

BPN: One Hidden Layer Back-Propagation Network. See "Back-Propagation Network"

Hidden layer: Intermediate layers of some architectures of neural networks. The hidden layer can be only one or can be several ones. It is generally the result of the input layer modified by the activation function and multiplied by the input layer weights.

Input layer: First layer of the neural network. It is generally the input pattern modified in some way to fit the network standards.

Layer: Group of artificial neurons. Biological researchers have discovered that human brain neurons work in groups. These groups have been simulated in a computer and are called "neuron layers."

Net: Artificial Neural Network. See "Artificial Neural Network"

Neural Layer: See "Layer"

Neural Network: Artificial Neural Network. See "Artificial Neural Network"

Nnet: or N-net: Artificial Neural Network. See "Artificial Neural Network"

OCR: Optical Character Recognition.

Optical Character Recognition: Technology that lets a scanner understand a written text and translate it into a computer text file.

Output layer: Last layer of the neural networks. Its value strongly depends on the network-specific architecture.

Parallel Hidden-Layers Network: A kind of neural network. It is similar to the BPN, but it has hidden layers in parallel. A BPN may have more than one hidden layer, but they are serial.

PHN: Parallel Hidden-Layers Network.

SAM: Self Associative Memory Network.

Self-Associative Memory Network: A kind of neural network. It was developed to receive defective patters (as text extracted from a Xerox machine copy in bad condition) and return them as correct ones. It could be seen as a special case of the SOM, where both patterns are the same.

Self-Organizing Map Network: Also known as Kohonen network. It was made to receive a pattern and match it with another one.

SOM: Self-Organizing Map Network.

Three-Layer Back-Propagation Network: See BPN

Weights: In this context, the weight of a layer is a series of attached values that simulate the strength of the synaptic connections. When a value is multiplied by its weight, it propagates an answer, which is affected by the strength of the weights.

Introduction

The new frontier: Internet.

This is one of the actual limits to the community of Neural Networks today.

Most of the works related to the field do not pay attention to the use of this technology. As a matter of fact, I felt that some elements were missing from the bibliography, such as a kind of vehicle that could be able to bridge these two worlds. That is how the main idea of this book came to light.

As stated earlier, *Web Neural Networks* was designed for students, amateur programmers, and other people who are interested in Neural Networks in conjunction with the Internet. This is a general target audience and will therefore include people with different levels of knowledge.

To ensure that these various levels of knowledge are addressed, this book is divided in several sections.

The introduction is a general overview of the material in the book, including an explanation of the various diagrams.

Part I, which includes Chapter 1, was written for those readers who have no previous knowledge of Neural Networks. It covers general concepts and provides basic definitions. Readers who are already somewhat familiar with this field of science may go directly to Part II (Chapters 2 and 3), which is the core of the book.

Part III includes Chapters 4, 5, and 6. Chapter 4 is a discussion of Neural Networks for the Internet—what they are and why we must use them. Also included are descriptions and explanations of the specific problems you will face when you design a Neural Network.

Symbols and procedures used in this book to make diagrams

For this book, I created a model of diagrams for Neural Network processes. To facilitate ease of understanding and writing, few elements are included. The shapes are simple and the environment is black and white so that one can write symbols using an ordinary word processor. No special graphic design software is needed to develop the symbols.

Graphic elements are divided into background and foreground symbols. The basic background symbols are provided in the following table.

Table A1.1

Basic Background Symbols

- Background symbols represent the environment of the Neural Network. Over them are the actions that must be executed to make the net run.

- The gray rectangle, which represents "the core network" (or "the net") itself, fixes the net limits. The net needs capture devices and human interaction to work. If a symbol is placed inside the gray rectangle, that symbol then belongs to the network. Conversely, if a symbol is outside the gray rectangle, then it is not part of the core network.

- The black square represents the space of an input-output device or a net-work operator.

- DB: This represents a database or recordset.

- An arrow, single- or double-headed, represents data flow.

Foreground symbols are a combination of the background shapes and their meanings. Table A1.2 shows the basic foreground symbols.

Table A1.2
Basic Foreground Symbols

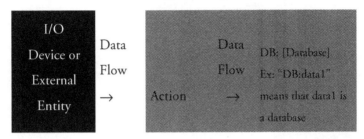

Peripheral input/output devices (Iodevs), also called External Beings or Entities, can be human beings or machines that provide information or collect the network outputs. Although Iodevs are not part of the network itself, they are necessary for the input patterns the net needs to operate. Any capture device, e.g., a scanner or digital camera attached to the net, is an Iodev, as is the net designer who receives the reports from the network. The information required can be provided in several formats, including a piece of paper, a diskette, a CD-ROM, an email, etc.

Actions (also called Processes) show the steps the network must perform to transform inputs to outputs. The most common actions are those taken to manipulate network data. These actions include data input, deletion and browsing.

Data Flows: When an arrow comes from or goes to a file or database, it refers to a reading/writing operation. The data is stored or retrieved from the database. An arrow entering or exiting the gray rectangle indicates a data input or output operation. The double-headed arrow indicates a reading and writing operation in a database. Some data is read. Other data is saved in the file.

Databases: Input layers, weights, outputs, and other data must be stored for later use. Although a database is generally used for permanent storage, it is common to work with computer arrays while the net runs. Computer arrays are faster than a database. Since the symbol does not differentiate between them, the net designer must choose one or the other.

Table A1.2 is a generic interpretation of a diagram.

Table A1.2
Generic interpretation of diagrams

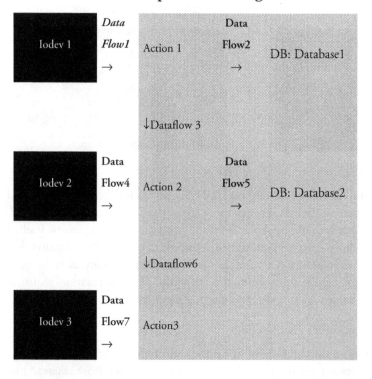

This diagram means that the net receives and propagates input patterns from Iodevs 1, 2, 3…These patterns generate actions 1, 2, 3. The output values are then stored in databases 1 and 2.

PART I

General Concepts about Neural Networks

CHAPTER 1

What is a Neural Network?

What is a Neural Network?

What do ordinary people think a Neural Network is?

What do they expect?

What do you think?

Recently, one of the distributors of my previous book received an email from a Canadian reader. I was surprised to see that he included the word "UFO" as a part of the subject of his email, so I asked him about this.

As a former member of a group investigating UFOs and paranormal sightings, he had grown tired of using low quality photos of white dots on a black background to explain these phenomena. After leaving the group, he became interested in Artificial Intelligence (AI) as a practical means through which contact might be made with other life forms…It is his belief that future contact with alien beings will begin in the laboratory with an Artificial Neural Network of this kind.

I explained to him that Neural Networks are just mathematical models that recognize patterns, and that thus far no one has been able to construct a Neural Network that thinks. We know that the human brain creates thoughts and complex behaviors using neurons and synaptic connections, but no one has discovered a way to reproduce this effect.

This email exchange made me think about how Neural Networks are perceived and what they represent to some people. For me, Neural Networks is a discipline involving abstract models (i.e., mathematical symbols and lines of programming code) through which computers can receive instructions. Yet for many people there is a magical quality in these processes and those who work with Neural Networks are seen as "wizards," which begs the question: Who is right? The scientists or the public?

Artificial Intelligence (AI) and Neural Networks

Opinions on AI vary. Some think that Neural Networks are not part of AI because they do not make the computer "think." Others are prepared to include Neural Networks in the field of AI. In my opinion, neither view can be accepted as absolute because we still do not know how a "thought" is produced. We do not know what "think" means. In the absence of this information, we are still unable to produce an algorithm to tell a computer to "be creative"—something on the order of BE_CREATIVE().

In this utopist environment, the only thing we should do to make the computer think and get an idea from it is to execute said function:

New idea = BE_CREATIVE().

This is science fiction, however, not science. From a scientific viewpoint, a Neural Network is the attempt to make inverse engineering of the brain. Traditional engineering begins with a plan that forms the basis for the creation of a machine or device. Inverse engineering starts with a machine or device and attempts to understand how it works.

A Neural Network is designed to simulate human brain behavior in a computer, reproducing, on a small scale, the brain's neurons and synaptic connections. The goal is to duplicate, in the artificial environment of a computer, the actions of the human brain or, in other words, to reproduce the human learning mechanism and pattern recognition in a manner that can be understood by a computer. Thus, one of the more interesting issues to be considered is the ability of the human brain to recognize patterns.

Pattern Recognition is the ability to see a complex image (a photograph, a motion picture) and to react accordingly...Digital computers use a binary logic of 2 values: 0-1 or True-False. Although this type of logic makes construction easier, it also makes it more difficult to process and recognize images, photos, planes, and drawings.

Some Uses of the Neural Networks

A small boy can look at a photograph and easily and immediately recognize his father or a family pet with 100 percent accuracy and effectiveness.

A computer, however, needs a great deal of programming to do the same thing, and even so, the result is not nearly as accurate or effective when compared to the precision of the human brain.

A computer with a pattern recognition system can take images from a video camera and, by itself, perform such tasks as recognizing company personnel and entrances and exits. This is a complicated process for the computer, however. For the human brain, it is quite simple.

Optical Character Recognition (OCR) programs are designed to achieve this type of pattern recognition.

OCR: Definition

An OCR program consists of software that tries to turn the digitalized image of a handwritten letter into a reasonable text file that can be used by the default text processor of a computer.

An OCR program can be designed on an algorithmic base (heuristic OCR program). This type of program is popular at the moment, but they have an appreciable degree of inaccuracy when the copy in the piece of paper is not perfect and presents or displays "noise"—that is to say when it is not an original one. (ex: a Xerox machine copy of a letter creates "dust" or small black dots in the copy when the original is not in excellent condition).

Thus, an OCR program based on pattern-recognition (such as the Neural Networks) might have the ability to ignore such noise in a way similar to any human brain easily distinguishing the text from the small dots in a Xerox copy of a handwritten letter.

Similarly, a system based on a Neural Network could recognize the digitalized image of a laser pulse refraction on an object (a painting, for example) and identify the quality of the painting based on that fact. This fact of comparing the discontinuities of the captured patterns to standard patterns allows the net to find out automatically which objects have not been painted properly. If the net is connected to a robot arm with a painting injector, it is possible then to order it to repaint the piece before mentioned.

In the same way, military applications also use this principle: The bounce of digital radar signals that sends an airplane to its opponent is recognized by a Neural Network which compares the pattern used with the ones of the enemy airplanes saved in its database. The aerodynamic properties and the fuselage shape of the airplane is digitalized and it is used to deduce whether an enemy plane is an ally or not. The same principle is used to detect a missile launch from an earth base, comparing the pattern of the foreground with the new pattern obtained when the missile is airborne. Fast information in modern warfare is so important that many of the decisions once made by human beings are now made by computers.

Each one of these items deserves individual research work. This fact gives us an idea about the scope of the Neural Network field.

Finally, it is possible to indicate that especially adaptable Neural Networks are suitable for scientific investigation of mathematical models with non-linear variables. In these models, the effects of the mutual interrelation of the variables make it difficult to solve them by using the traditional algorithmic methods.

Brain as a Process

Our human brain can be seen as a process (thought) that turns inputs (mainly sensorial) into outputs (actions). We can graphically observe this process in table RN001.

Table RN001

Process of thoughts considering mind functions

Human Brain

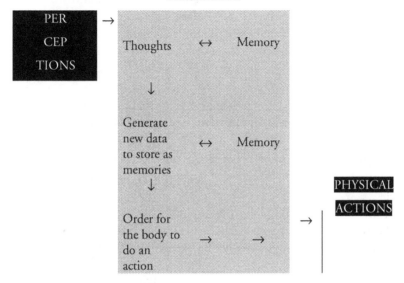

There are diverse stimuli that flow to the brain, which are called "perceptions." The human being is a system that uses sensorial inputs for its process of thought. The word "perception" includes not only the stimuli that the environment projects to the five senses but also the illusions and ideas that the subject's mind itself can discern.

The brain is stimulated by a simultaneous interrelation of perceptions, which activates the process we have called "thought." In order to do that, it requires some data ("experiences") stored in the memory of the individual, which can be seen as a file or database, called "Memories" in this context.

The process of thought has a kind of sub-product, that is the creation of data to be stored, which will be transformed into new memories. It implies the following:

Thought is a recursive process that uses memory both as an input and as an output. The cumulative effect of this behavior is usually called "experience."

Therefore, it is possible to consider "thought" as a reading and writing process of the "memory" database. In the middle of these facts, we find another sub-process: the brain has to prepare an output in the form of an order given to the body so as to do something. If the process of thought finishes with the idea "I want to get an apple," the brain has to order the arm and then hand to catch the apple.

This action can be physical or psychic. In the first case, certain muscles of the body are programmed to move themselves in a definite direction.

Example: An increase in room temperature causes in the individual the perception of heat and this directs his actions towards the ingestion of water to eliminate his thirst.

In the second case, the perception can be focused toward the recovery of a memory. In other words, it goes on a search in the memory database.

Example: The perception of a floral aroma may lead us to remember a pleasant past experience in a field of flowers.

The brain is composed of a vast assembly of cells called neurons, which are interrelated among each other via electrical impulses, by means of synaptic connections. The neurons are placed in the form of a network where each one of them is a node, interlaced by means of connections that transmit electrical signals. A neuron can receive and transmit electrical signals from and towards several other neurons. Table RN002 shows this process.

Table RN002

Environment of a neuron

Neuron

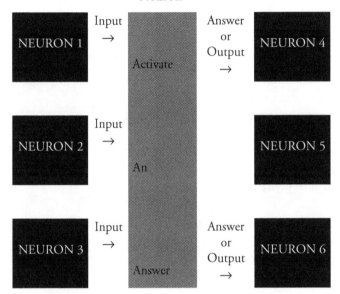

From a physical point of view, thought consists of a series of electrical interactions among the neurons, which have the following behavior:

a) Receive signals: Each neuron receives one or several electrical messages from the adjacent neurons.

b) Condition the unloading: The neuron acts like a transit system that takes the energy transferred to it and decides whether it has to activate itself to send an answer or not.

c) Unload (give an answer) and reinforce connections: The energy is expelled towards the adjacent neurons to which it is connected. At the same time, the synaptic connections are reinforced. This means that a preference system is set up to direct the answers. The connections recently used to transmit an answer are stronger than the others. The next time the same impulse comes to the original neuron, the output will be directed using these stronger connections.

Programming the Neuron

If we use a metaphor, and we think of a neuron as if it were a piece of software, then we could say that a neuron is a program that conducts the following tasks:

1. Get electrical impulses from its neighbors
2. Decide which neurons will be chosen to unload the energy
3. Select a neuron from the ones previously chosen in point 2. It will be called "output neuron"
4. Unload energy towards the output neuron
5. Reinforce its connection with this neuron
6. Return to point 3 and loop until all the energy is unloaded
7. Return to point 1and start again

This process continues until every neuron of the chosen ones has received its answer. In the human body, there are some neurons that are also connected to a nervous terminal, (eyes, medulla, nerves, etc.) which activate the corresponding actions.

If we examine the program, we can deduce that (at any time) there are groups of neurons, which work together at the same time. (They are the ones chosen from a previous group of neurons.) We may think of these groups as layers of neurons. We will then have different neuron layers that will have the function of increasing or decreasing the strength of the neural paths. (Strength of a neural path: probability that a certain path could be selected next time if a similar impulse excites the neuron.)

These facts are consistent with brain physiology research, which agrees with the existence of different specialized zones of the brain that perform the specific neural tasks.

Memory

We can say that Memory consists (from this approach) in the sum of strengths or preferences (called "weights") corresponding to the connections of a layer of related neurons. In this context, the weight of a layer is a series of attached values that simulates the strength of the synaptic connections. When a value is multiplied by its weight, it propagates an answer that affects the strength of its neighbors.

As a result, the activation of the neurons by a nervous impulse causes an emission of energy that flows through neuron layers and provokes the sensation of a "memory."

As a matter of fact, the same element (the neuron) acts like a signal driver, as memory, on one hand, and as a decision manager, on the other. From our point of view, we have to speak of data-bus for the synaptic connection, which manages software to decide when it has to load and unload the electric signals that flow in the computer.

Axioms to make possible a kind of simulation of the biological process

Thus, we will need some axioms to simulate these processes using computers. Without them, the idea of an artificial Neural Network would have no sense.

Main axiom

We do not have to care about the physical substance which neurons are made of (DNA versus silicon). It is not important. What it counts is the function.

Neurons, like living creatures, are composed of interlaced carbon atom strings. Nevertheless, the chemical composition of the same ones is not a determining factor at the time of trying to duplicate them. The important point is its function, not the raw material. If we believe in this axiom, we can conclude that it is possible to create an artificial neuron simulating its functions in an artificial (non-human) device like a computer. If we do not use this assumption, the study of artificial Neural Networks would have to be suspended since it would not be possible to perform them.

This axiom leads us to think about brain webs like kinds of "carbon networks." Devices created in another material can simulate some of their functions.

A wheel can be made of wood, metal, or vulcanized rubber, but it is always a wheel.

Secondary axiom

It is possible to recognize patterns using the interactions between the network nodes.

This means that if we have an artificial substitute of the neurons, and we use among them a similar mechanism of interaction as the one used by the human brain, some of the abstract brain functions will be duplicated or simulated.

If we did not have this axiom, it would not be possible to continue with the N-Net research since there would not be a way to reproduce the behavior using artificial neurons.

Considering the existence of the aforementioned theorems, we should now set out the computing equivalence of the elements previously seen.

The following table shows an equivalence between the artificial elements and the biological ones to reproduce a neuronal layer:

TABLE RN003
Artificial Equivalence between Biological and Artificial elements

BIOLOGICAL ELEMENT	ARTIFICIAL ELEMENT
NEURON	Network node=
	Ram memory +
	Hard Disk space +
	Neural network software
SENSORIAL INPUT	Digital Images and signals
	Computer Files
BEHAVIOR (SENSORIAL OUTPUT)	Creation of computer files containing the output data
	Execution of a predefined computer program
	Activation of robotic interfaces
SYNAPTIC CONNECTIONS	Transferences between the memory positions
	Values and weights of the data passed from node to node

PART II

Neural Networks:
Usual architectures

CHAPTER 2

What is an architecture?

One of the most important points to consider when we need to program a Neural Network is the design of a suitable network architecture. This is one of the aspects where we can appreciate the work of the network designer. The chosen network architecture gives a mark, a "signature," which talks about the author. We can find as many architectures as there are designers. Each person will try to add some element to his creation that will allow the network to have a special characteristic.

However, there exist some standard network models that can be used as testing functions. If the prototype of our network does not have a better performance than these models, then the effort must be continued. If the new network improves the previous efforts to reach the goal, then we can say that it has reached a worthy solution for the work.

This book was not conceived as an encyclopedia. In other words, it is not the intention of the author to show every architecture that exists (It would take 400–500 pages to do that. The idea of this book is to make this work as simple as possible.), but to show the most popular ones, for you to understand what they are and the differences among them.

BPN: Backward Propagation Network

The Back Propagation Network with a hidden-layer, or BPN, or Back-prop (3-layer Back Propagation Network) is perhaps the most classic and popular structure that exists, and it is frequently used as a reference network. It consists of three main **layers**: (a layer contains the values of a group of related variables in a particular moment)

In a BPN we will find 3 basic elements:

The **Input layer**: It contains the original pattern to be recognized.

The **Hidden layer**: The initial weights and an output function (we will call it here **activation function**) are assigned to it. Here again we will use the concept of **weight**. (For the first time, we will use random values as weights.) When we multiply the input layer by the weights and we apply the activation function, we will get, as a result of it, hidden layer values.

The **Output layer**: The output layer has also an attached weight layer and it may also have an activation function. Multiplying the hidden layer by its weights and applying the activation function, we get the output layer values.

Here we will talk about the **output function**, but you can think of it as something similar to the activation function.

Basic Scheme of a 3-layer BPN

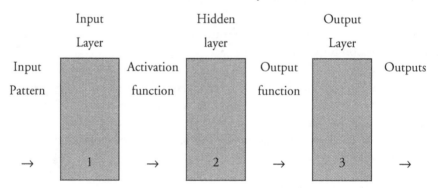

In other words:

$$\text{Layer}_1 = \text{activation function}(\text{Layer}_0 \times \text{weights})$$

In a BPN we will have the following:

Input Layer = Conversion of the input pattern into a binary string
Hidden Layer = Activation function(**Input Layer ×** input-layer weights)
Output Layer = Output function(**Hidden Layer ×** hidden-layer weights)

The following table shows the data flow scheme of a BPN with a hidden layer…

3-Layer Back Propagation Network

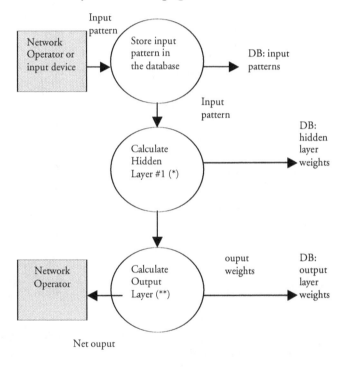

(*) Hidden layer = Multiply input pattern by its weights and apply
the activation function to it. In other words:
Hidden Layer = activation function (input pattern * weights)

(**) Output Layer = output function (hidden layer * output weights)

Each layer has its inputs and its outputs, so we will talk here about concepts such as "The input-layer output." This could be complicated to understand. The following table shows us this sequence.

Sequence of Inputs and Outputs in a BPN

	(1)	Input pattern
	(2)	Weights #1
Net value for the input layer	(3)	$\Sigma(1) * (2)$
Output from hidden layer	(4)	activation function[(3)]
	(5)	Weights #2
Net value for the output-layer	(6)	$\Sigma(4) * (5)$
Net Output	(7)	output function[(6)]

BPN: Equations involved

As I have already said, my aim is to make this book as simple as possible. So I will try to use as few equations as possible.

However, if you do not like mathematics, feel free to skip this section. I have written this book in such a way that I expect the basic ideas to be understood anyway.

Suppose we have two arrays: one for the inputs and one for the initial weights.

The input array has N elements:

$$Inputs_{(i)} = (input_{i1}, input_{i2}, ..., input_{in})$$

We will need as many input arrays as patterns we use, so we can also think about them as a unique two-dimensional array.

The array that contains the weights also has two dimensions. The first dimension represents the number of hidden nodes, and the second one, the number of elements of the input patterns:

$$Weights_{(ij)} = (weight_{i1}, weights_{i2}, ..., weight_{in})$$

As there are other weights in the BPN, we should label them with a more specific name such as:

$$Layer1\_Weights_{(ij)} = (weight_{i1}, weights_{i2}, .., weight_{in})$$

To make this denomination shorter, we can just say:

$$\alpha_{(ij)} = (weight_{i1}, weights_{i2}, ..., weight_{in})$$
$$\alpha = Layer1\_weights$$

Each element of the array can be identified as:

$$\alpha(ij) = \text{it means the element number "}j\text{" of } \alpha(i)$$

When we multiply the inputs by their weights, we will get **Net inputs**. The net input of the "i" unit will be:

$$NetInput(i) = \sum_{j=1}^{n} \alpha(ij) * inputs(j)$$

After that, we have to calculate the output of the hidden layer. We need to use the activation function to do it.

$$OutputHL_{(i)} = \text{Activation Function}(NetInput_{(i)})$$

Later on, we will discuss the activation function. Let us suppose now that we use a hyperbolic tangent (Tanh) function as our activation function. The equations will look like this:

$$\beta_{(i)} = Tanh(\sum_{j=1}^{n} \alpha_{(ij)} * inputs_{(j)})$$

$Note: \beta = Outputs.from.hidden-layer$

This will give us the output of the hidden-layer.

Now, we have to calculate the following values of the net. The procedure is similar. We use the outputs of the hidden-layer as our new inputs, and we repeat the procedure. So we have the following:

a) Our output for the hidden-layer

b) The output layer has its own weights, so we will also have the following:

$$\delta_{(ij)} = (weight_{i1}, weight_{i2},.., weight_{in})$$

$\delta = weights.from.output-layer$

The output layer will be calculated with the same algorithm as the previous net inputs, so we will have the following:

$$Net\_values_{(i)} = \sum_{j=1}^{n} \beta_{(ij)} * \delta_{(i)}$$

After that, we have to calculate the output of the BPN. We need to use the activation function to do it.

$$BPNOutput_{(i)} = \text{Output Function}(Net\_values_{(i)})$$

The output function can be the same as the activation function, or it can be some other one.

Tanh() is a function that returns a value between 1 and -1.

$$-1 <= Tanh(x) <= 1$$

If we use it again as an output function, we will have the following:

$$BPNOutput(i) = Tanh(\sum_{j=1}^{n} \beta(ij) * \delta(j))$$

BPN: Forward & Back Propagation

In the field of Neural Networks, we use the word "propagation" to refer to the process of calculating the values of one layer and sending them on to the next.

You can propagate the network in two ways: from inputs to outputs, or from outputs to inputs. We use the terms "Forward" and "Back" propagation to refer to these effects. When the network finds an answer, forward propagation is completed.

BPN—How does the N-Net learn?: Training & Executing the net

Back-Prop works in two ways. First of all, before it works properly, we have to "train" it. What is that? Very simple: Back-Prop recognizes a series of patterns that must be loaded in advance. The net must be trained to recognize these patterns.

The weights must be "trained" before they are able to recognize the patterns (this process is equivalent to the "memory" of the human brain). To train the network means that we must place the proper weights in the net so a specific input pattern could be connected with a specific output answer. This process is equivalent to increase or to attenuate the synaptic connections among the neurons.

How do we train the net? We use several elements to do this.

- Input Patterns & Output Expected Patterns
- Forward Propagation
- Error Detection Method or Algorithm
- Back Propagation

Let us suppose we want the net to recognize eight different patterns: First of all we have to enter these patterns in the net database. Then we have to enter the output expected patterns. For example: We save pattern #1 in the database, and then we order the net that this pattern has to correspond to output "one." (This is the expected output. It is the value we are expecting to be returned by the net as output when we introduce pattern #1.)

Example: Let us suppose we enter this input pattern.

Input Layer 1

0, 1, 0, 1, 1, 0, 0, 1, 0, 0, 1, 0, 0, 1, 0, 0, 1, 0

We also enter initial weights to the net.

Input Layer Weights

0, 0, 1, 0, 1, 0, 1, 1, 0, 1, 1, 0, 1, 1, 0, 0, 1, 1

THIS IS A RANDOMLY SELECTED STRING. IT HAS NO MEANING AT THIS MOMENT.

Once we have entered the patterns, we start the training of the net. We start with the first pattern and we forward propagate it. Let us remember that when we propagate, we use the real weights of the net. The first time we train a pattern, the initial weights will be incorrect, so the net will surely give us a wrong answer. We will call it "net output." So, up to now we have four elements: input pattern, initial weights, expected output value, and net output.

Then, we have to measure the extent of the error in some way. Here we need a method, or a learning algorithm, that could do this task for us.

BPN: Getting suitable weights

This procedure varies according to the network architecture we are using and the design of it. One of the ordinary methods consists of the fixing of proper weights according to some error-minimization algorithm.

There are different methods to calculate the error. The simplest method is to think that the error is the difference between the Expected Output for the pattern, and the Net output.

$$\text{Error} = (\text{Expected Output - Net Output})$$

In other words, the error of the "n" element will be:

$$\text{Error}_{(n)} = \text{Expected Output}_{(n)} - \text{Net Output}_{(n)}$$

Or

$$\varepsilon_{(n)} = \text{Expected Output}_{(n)} - \text{Net Output}_{(n)}$$

Many net designers prefer to use some kind of method that attenuates this difference. In any discussion of methods to minimize the error, the "Generalized Delta Rule" is often mentioned. An example would be learning an algorithm that postulates that errors can be calculated as follows:

$$\text{Error} = (\text{Expected Output - Net output}) * \text{Net output} * (1 - \text{Net output})$$

In other words, the error for the unit "i" will be as follows:

$$\text{Error}_{(i)} = (\text{Expected Output}_{(i)} - \text{Net output}_{(i)}) * \text{Net output}_{(i)} * (1 - \text{Net output}_{(i)})$$

Or

$$\varepsilon_{(i)} = \text{Error}_{(i)}$$

Once we have calculated the error (using our favorite learning algorithm), we have to update the weights.

Then our new weights will be like these ones:

$$New\ weights = Old\ weights * error$$

$$Or$$

$$New\ \alpha = Old\ \alpha * \varepsilon$$

$$New\ \delta = Old\ \delta * \varepsilon$$

So, the algorithms to calculate our new weights for the element "i" will be like these:

$$New\ \alpha_{(ij)} = Old\ \alpha_{(ij)} * \varepsilon_{(i)}$$

$$New\ \alpha_{(ij)} = Old\ \alpha_{(ij)} * \varepsilon_{(i)}$$

If we think in terms of the iterations of the BPN, we can say the following:

$$\alpha_{(iteration)} = \alpha_{(iteration-1)} * \varepsilon_{(i)}$$

$$\delta_{(iteration)} = \delta_{(iteration-1)} * \varepsilon_{(i)}$$

Summary

Let's have a short summary here:

In the previous paragraphs, we have said that:

a)
$$\alpha_{(ij)} = (weight_{i1}, weights_{i2},.., weight_{in})$$

b)
$$\delta_{(ij)} = (weight_{i1}, weight_{i2},.., weight_{in})$$
$$\delta = weights.\ from.output-layer$$

c)

$\varepsilon_{(i)} = (\text{Expected Output}_{(i)} - \text{Net output}_{(i)}) * \text{Net output}_{(i)} * (1 - \text{Net output}_{(i)}).$

It has already been said that thought is a recursive process. At the moment, we have to start a process of this kind.

Once we know the extent of the error, we use the back-propagation of the net. Remember that now we are moving from Outputs to Inputs.

The old weights are replaced by these new weights and then the BPN is executed again using these new values. We will then get a new value for the error. Comparing this error with the previous one, we can set the **trend.**

BPN: Setting the trend

Using the error values, we have to recalculate the weights of the network in a pre-defined way. If the error is positive, then we must decrease the values of the weights. On the other hand, if the error is negative, said values must be increased.

The designer changes the weights in a given direction (increasing or decreasing the values in a small percentage) and again executes the network. If the new error is not increased, the tendency is towards the minimization of the error. On the other hand, the trend must be reverted. Once the trend is set, the designer chooses the minimum error that the net must accept to work properly. This is a given value and depends on the accuracy that is required in the pattern recognition. Example: The designer may say "The network may have an error of 0,05 percent or less."

Using these new weights, we have to go on with the iterative process: We again apply forward propagation, which gives us a new net output and a new error. We again use back propagation and we recalculate the weights using these new error values. This is done until the error becomes insignificant.

At this point, the net output is equal to the expected output (with a minimum difference). So, if you entered pattern #1, and you expected that the net answer were "0.99" or "99%," the answer will be that one.

These iteration processes must be repeated with the rest of the input patterns. If we had eight input patterns, the iteration has to run eight times. As a new layer is entered, an iterative process is necessary where the old patterns must be reintroduced again, to avoid the old associated weights being lost. In a human being, we could say that each time new knowledge is given to the net, the old knowledge may be forgotten, so the old knowledge must be reinforced. The new weights must be able to recognize not only the new patterns but also the old ones.

The final weight values are then stored in the database of the BPN to be used as input weight values for the execution of the Neural Network. At this point it is said that the network is already trained, and therefore qualified for the recognition of patterns. Anyway, the net will only recognize those patterns that are similar to the trained ones.

This procedure must be repeated for each pattern. In other words, the net has to be trained for every pattern that it has to recognize. When a new pattern appears, the net has to be retrained again. The training of the network can be compared to the learning process in a human being.

The network administrator may train the net previously to be executed (for example, at the end of the previous day) or online (just before it needs to be used). As it may take much time, the first alternative is recommended.

Once the net is trained, we can execute the program (i.e., use it). We execute the net when we enter a new pattern, and we forward propagate. If the pattern is one of the eight original ones, the net will recognize it, and will tell us which one it is. If it is another pattern, the net will tell us there is no match.

BPN training: Summary

Training is a process that has to be done each time you want to teach the net to recognize a new pattern. This is done by the Neural Network administrator.

Execution is a process that has to be done each time you introduce a pattern and want the net to tell you if it is recognized or not. It is performed by a Neural Network user.

Activation and Output functions

In order to calculate the values to propagate one layer to the next one, we must start with the values of the current layer. Then, we must apply the *activation function* we have chosen to the data. At this point we are able to multiply it by the respective weights.

An **activation function** is a mathematical function that is applied to the original data and returns a result that is multiplied by the proper weights to generate the input for the next layer. This weight simulates the strength or weakness of the synaptic connection among the neurons. When the value of the associated weight is important, we have the simulation of a strong connection. When it is irrelevant we will have a weak connection. A weight with zero value means a null connection. The **output function** converts the net output into a suitable format. For example, if our output is in a range of [-1,1], we can use the hyperbolic tangent as our output function, because it returns us a value between -1 and 1. If we do not care about this fact, we can omit the output function, or use f(x) = x as a function. The output function can be the same as the activation function, but this is not a fixed rule.

Choosing an Activation Function

If the selected activation function were the hyperbolic tangent, we could then have: f(x) = tanh(x). The hyperbolic tangent is a function that looks like an "S" and returns as follows:

- -1 if x < -10. Example: tanh(-10) = -1
- a negative number between 0 and -1 if x < 0 and x > -10
- 0 if x is 0. Example: tanh(0) = 0
- a positive number between 0 and -1 if x > 0 and x < 10
- 1 if x > 10. Example: tanh(10) = 1

The choosing of a suitable activation function is a craftsman-like task of the network designer, who shows us here his own personal touch. Two different networks made for the same purpose will be different from each other in the choice of their activation functions. This fact gives the activation functions the status of "signature" or "personal touch" of the designer. Some of them use the function to convert the data into normalized serials, as could be the use of the sigmoid or sinus functions. Some others apply elaborated handmade functions.

Usual Activation Functions

The objectives of an activation function will vary depending on the objectives and degree of transformation expected by the network designer. The simplest ones only try to standardize the data or convert it into binary strings. As it is said in the body of the book, the election of the activation function is a craftsman choice of the network designer. None of them is more recommended than the others for all purposes. Each case must be seen independently.

In general, during the first training process, several functions may be proved to check which one has a better performance. In table A4.1 we can see some usual activation functions

TABLE A4.1
Usual activation Functions

Activation Functions	
Logistic Function	$Y= 1/(1+e^{(-x)})$
Decimal to Boolean	$Y = dec2bool(x)$
Decimal to Bipolar	$Y=dec2bip(x)$
Cosine	$Y=cos(x)$
Hyperbolic tangent of X	$Y=tanh(x)$
Hyperbolic tangent of 1,5 X	$Y=tanh(1.5 * x)$
Sine	$Y=sin(x)$
Symmetrical Sigmoid	$Y=2/(1+exp(-x))^{-1}$
Gaussian	$Y=exp(-x^2)$
Complement of Gaussian	$Y=1-exp(-x^2)$

- *Logistic Function:*

One of the standard functions used is the sigmoid or logistic function as a default activation function. The function may be used in its original design

$$Y = 1/(1 + e^{(-x)}),$$

or in any of the versions thereof, like:

$$Y = 1/(1 + e^{(-x1 * x2)}) +x3$$

Programmed in ASP:

```
Function Sigmoid (sigmoid01)
e = 2.718281828459050
sigmoid = 1/(1 + e^(sigmoid01))
End function
```

- *Decimal to Boolean Function:*

This is a simple function that turns input data into format (**True/False**), symbolized as **0 = True—1 = False.**

Example: If all we need to know is the sign of the numbers (positive or negative), it is advisable to turn all positive data into 1 and all the negative values into 0. In this way, a better process is obtained.

The algorithm for this function must do these actions:

- *Input a decimal number*
- *If the number is smaller than or equal to 0 then return 0*
- *Or else return 1*

We see that the algorithm consists of a condition that returns 1 or 0 depending on the value of the given input number.

The programming of this algorithm in ASP is:

```
Function Dec2bool(deci)
Dec2bool = 1
If deci <= 0 Then Dec2bool = 0
End Function
```

This is a useful function. However, the zero/one format has this disadvantage: When we multiply any number by zero the result is zero, which is the reason why the changes in the weights of the network become abrupt.

In order to avoid this effect, it is common to use a variant of the binary system, which uses [1 and -1] instead of [0 and 1]. This system is called "**bipolar**" and it has the advantage that there are no null values when we multiply. The following function is another version of the previous one using bipolar values.

The algorithm for this function must do the following actions:

- *Input a decimal number*
- *If the number is smaller than or equal to 0.5 then return -1*
- *Or else return 1*

In ASP the code is:

```
Function Dec2bip (deci)
Dec2bip = 1
If deci <= 0.5 Then Dec2bip = -1
End Function
```

Other usual function is Only-Positive()

It returns null (or 0) if the parameter is <= 0.
Otherwise, it returns 1

In ASP the code is:

```
Function Only-positive (deci)
Only-positive = 0
If deci > 0 Then Only-positive = 1
End Function
```

Another useful function is the *Binary-to-decimal* one.

Example: This function returns the decimal number equivalent to a given binary value. It is used in those cases where we must turn the binary results of the net into its decimal equivalency.

In ASP the code is:

```
Function Binary-to-decimal (b2d)
b2d = Trim(b2d)
bin2d = 0
lencadena = Len(b2d)
For i = 0 lencadena To -1
zeroone = Val(Mid(b2d, lencadena - i, 1))
bin2d = bin2d + zeroone * (2 ^ i)
Next
binary-to-decimal = bin2d
End Function
```

BPN: Mathematical Equations to make a 3-layer Back-Prop

First of all, we must create an array to store the input pattern, whose number of elements agrees with the number of elements of this pattern.

Equation 1

$$Inputs_{(i)} = (input_{i1}, input_{i2}, ..., input_{in})$$

Secondly, we must also create an array to store the hidden layer whose number of elements is equal to the number of elements of the input layer.

Equation 2

$$Weights_{(ij)} = (weight_{i1}, weights_{i2}, ..., weight_{in})$$

or

$$\alpha_{(ij)} = (weight_{i1}, weights_{i2}, ..., weight_{in})$$

$\alpha = Layer1\_weights$

Thirdly, we must calculate the net input of the input-layer.

Equation 3

$$NetInput(i) = \sum_{j=1}^{n} \alpha(ij) * inputs(j)$$

Forth, we have to calculate the result of the activation function, using the net inputs as a dependent variable.

Equation 4

$$OutputHL_{(i)} = \text{Activation Function}(NetInput_{(i)})$$

$$\beta(i) = Tanh(\sum_{j=1}^{n} \alpha(ij) * inputs(j))$$

$Note: \beta = Outputs.from.hidden-layer$

The hidden layer also has weights, so we have to create an array to store them.

Equation 5

$$\delta(ij) = (weight_{i1}, weight_{i2}, ..., weight_{in})$$

$\delta = weights.from.output-layer$

Equation 6

Next, the net value of the output layer will be calculated in the following way:

$$Net\_values(i) = \sum_{j=1}^{n} \beta(ij) * \delta(i)$$

Then we have to apply the activation function to this equation to get the BPN output:

Equation 7

$$BPNOutput_{(i)} = \text{Output Function}(Net\_values_{(i)})$$

If we use the hyperbolic tangent function to do it, we will have the following function:

$$BPNOutput(i) = Tanh(\sum_{j=1}^{n} \beta_{(ij)} * \delta_{(j)})$$

Equation 8

Now we have to measure the error the net returned. In order to do it, we will use the following function:

$$\varepsilon_{(n)} = \text{Expected Output}_{(n)} - \text{Net output}_{(n)}$$

Otherwise, we can use a learning algorithm such as the Generalized Delta Rule, which calculates the error as:

$$\varepsilon_{(i)} = (\text{Expected Output}_{(i)} - \text{Net output}_{(i)}) * \text{Net output}_{(i)} * (1 - \text{Net output}_{(i)}).$$

Equation 9

To train the net, we start an iterative process where both weights are replaced by the previous weight multiplied by the error. This continues until the error is insignificant. The network operator sets up this value.

$$\text{Current } \alpha_{(ij)} = \text{Previous } \alpha_{(ij)} * \varepsilon_{(i)}$$

$$\text{Current } \alpha_{(ij)} = \text{Previous } \alpha_{(ij)} * \varepsilon_{(i)}$$

When this iteration is ready, the net is trained. Finally, all we have to do is to enter a sample pattern, and run a forward propagation to see if the net recognizes it or not.

-------------0-------------

BPN: Execution and training of the Neural Network

The following tables show the two operative "modes" of the back-propagation network. Remember that the net has to be "trained" to "teach" it the patterns. We have to retrain it each time a new pattern appears. Once the net is trained, we can use it to recognize them. This mode is called "execution mode."

Execution of a Neural Network (Execution mode)

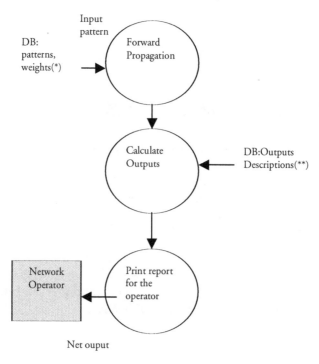

Net ouput

<table>
<tr><td>

(*) DB: Database of the system that contains the input patterns and weights

(**) DB: Database of the system that contains the descriptions that correspond to each output. Ex: if the net returns the value of 0.5, the description of it could be a message that says: "This is pattern #1"

</td></tr>
</table>

Table RN005

Neural Network Training System

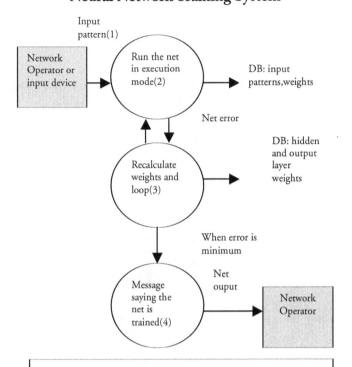

(1) Input pattern = Here the net loads all the sample patterns and the expected outputs for each one:

(2) The net returns an output value that is not exact. The difference between this value and the expected output value is the error of the network

(3) Based in the error, the output layer weights are recalculated and these new values are saved in the database. The net is executed again and this loop continues until the net error is minimum

(4) Once the error is minimum, the net sends a message to the operator saying that it is trained

4L-BPN:Four-Layer Back Propagation Network

It has a similar configuration to the 3-layer BPN (we will call it 3L-BPN here), but it has one added extra hidden layer. Therefore, it has one input layer, two hidden layers, and one output layer.

This is also a standard testing network to compare its performance with our own prototype. The following tables show the basic scheme and the data-flow of a 4-Layer Back-Propagation Network.

Basic Scheme of a 4-Layer BPN

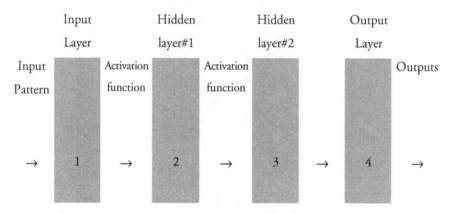

Table A5.4

4-Layer Back Propagation Network

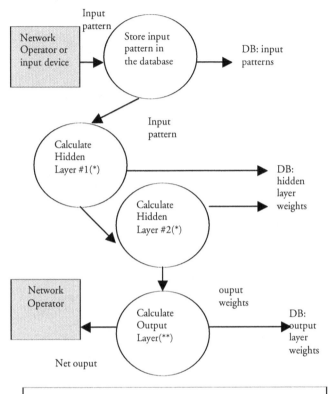

(*) Hidden layer #1 =
     activation function#1 (input pattern) * weights #1
     Hidden layer #2 =
     activation function#1 (hidden layer#1) * weights #2

(**) Output layer =
     activation function #1 (hidden layer values) * output weights

Sequence of Inputs and Outputs in a 4L–BPN

	(1)	Input pattern
	(2)	Weights #1
Net value for the input layer	(3)	$\Sigma(1) * (2)$
Output from the first hidden layer	(4)	activation function#1[(3)]
	(5)	Weights #2
Net value from the fist hidden layer	(6)	$\Sigma(4) * (5)$
Output from the 2nd hidden layer	(7)	activation function#2[(6)]
	(8)	Weights #3
Net value for the output-layer	(9)	$\Sigma(7) * (8)$
Net Output	(10)	Output function[(9)]

Most of this net uses the same structure as the 3L back-prop, so we start again with two arrays, one for the inputs, and one for the initial weights.

$$Inputs(i) = (input_{i1}, input_{i2}, ..., input_{in})$$

and

$$\alpha(ij) = (weight_{i}1, weights_{i}2, ..., weight_{i}n)$$
$\alpha = Layer1\_weights$

Again, when we multiply the inputs by their weights, we will have the Net inputs. The net input of the "i" unit will be the following:

$$NetInput(i) = \sum_{j=1}^{n} \alpha(ij) * inputs(j)$$

Here we find the first difference: As we have two hidden layers, each of them may have the same activation function or a different one. For example, the activation function#1 could be y = tanh(), as we have seen before, and the second one could be the sigmoid function y = 1/(1 + e$^{(-x)}$) (shown in the paragraphs named "usual activation functions" of the 3L-BPN section).

$$OutputHL_{(i)} = \text{Activation Function\#1}(NetInput_{(i)})$$

Here we suppose that our first hidden layer uses the hyperbolic tangent (Tanh) function as our activation function, so the equations will look like this one:

$$\beta(i) = Tanh(\sum_{j=1}^{n} \alpha(ij) * inputs(j))$$
Note: β = Outputs. from.hidden–layer

This will give us the output of the first hidden-layer.

At this point you will have the biggest difference: we have to calculate the extra hidden layer. We have to multiply the outputs of the previous hidden layer by the weights of the second hidden layer. Thus, we will get the following:

$$\phi(ij) = (weight_{i}1, weights_{i}2, ..., weight_{i}n)$$
$\phi = second.hidden–layer.weights$

The net input of the "i" unit will be as follows:

$$2hlNetInput(i) = \sum_{j=1}^{n} \phi(ij) * Netinputs(j)$$

We get the output of the second hidden layer by calculating the result of the second activation function.

$$Output2HL_{(i)} = \text{Activation Function\#2}(2hlNetInput_{(i)})$$

If our second hidden layer uses the sigmoid function as its activation function, the equation will be the following:

$$\beta(i) = Sigmoid(\sum_{j=1}^{n} \phi(ij) * Netinputs(j))$$

Note: $\phi = Outputs.\,from.second.hidden{-}layer$

From now on, the procedure is equal to the 3-layer BPN. We use the outputs of the second hidden-layer as our new inputs, and we repeat the procedure. So we will have the following:

a) Our output from the second hidden-layer:

b) The output layer has its own weights, so we will also have the following:

$$\delta(ij) = (weight\,i1,\, weight\,i2,..,\, weight\,in)$$

$\delta = weights.\,from.output{-}layer$

The output layer will be calculated with the same algorithm as the previous net inputs, so we will have the following:

$$4LBPN - Net\_values(i) = \sum_{j=1}^{n} \beta(ij) * \delta(i)$$

After that, we have to calculate the output of the 4L-BPN. We need to use the activation function to do it.

$$\textit{4L-BPNOutput}_{(i)} = \text{Output Function}(\textit{4LBPN - Net\_values}_{(i)})$$

The output function can be the same as the activation function, or it can be some other one.

If we use the sigmoid function again as the output function, we will have the following:

$$4L - BPNOutput(i) = Sigmoid(\sum_{j=1}^{n} \beta_{(ij)} * \delta_{(j)})$$

The error is calculated either using the Delta Rule or any other learning algorithm. We will use here:

$$\text{Error} = (\text{Expected Output - Net output})$$

So, the error of the "n" element will be the following:

$$\varepsilon_{(n)} = \text{Expected Output}_{(n)} - \text{Net output}_{(n)}$$

Here, there is again a difference between 3L-BPN and 4L-BPN. In the previous net, we had only two weight arrays to recalculate:

$$\textit{Current } \alpha_{(ij)} = \textit{Previous } \alpha_{(ij)} * \varepsilon_{(i)}$$

$$\textit{Current } \delta_{(ij)} = \textit{Previous } \delta_{(ij)} * \varepsilon_{(i)}$$

Here, we have one extra layer to calculate, so our iteration process will affect these two layers plus the hidden one:

$$\textit{Current } \alpha_{(ij)} = \textit{Previous } \alpha_{(ij)} * \varepsilon_{(i)}$$

$$\textit{Current } \beta_{(ij)} = \textit{Previous } \beta_{(ij)} * \varepsilon_{(i)}$$

$$\textit{Current } \delta_{(ij)} = \textit{Previous } \delta_{(ij)} * \varepsilon_{(i)}$$

Once the net is trained, we have to enter a sample pattern, and make a forward propagation to see whether the net recognizes it or not.

4L-BPN: Mathematical equations to make a 4-layer Back-prop

First of all, we must create an array to store the input pattern, whose number of elements agrees with the number of elements of this pattern.

Forward Propagation

Equation 1

$$Inputs(i) = (input_{i1}, input_{i2}, ..., input_{in})$$

We must also create an array to store the hidden layer whose number of elements is equal to the number of elements of the input layer.

Equation 2

$$Weights(ij) = (weight_{i1}, weights_{i2}, .., weight_{in})$$

or

$$\alpha(ij) = (weight_{i1}, weights_{i2}, .., weight_{in})$$
$$\alpha = Layer1\_weights$$

Next, we must calculate the net input of the input-layer

Equation 3

$$NetInput(i) = \sum_{j=1}^{n} \alpha(ij) * inputs(j)$$

At this point, we have to calculate the result of the activation function, using the net inputs as a dependent variable.

Equation 4

$OutputHL_{(i)}$ = Activation Function($NetInput_{(i)}$)

$$\beta_{(i)} = Tanh(\sum_{j=1}^{n} \alpha_{(ij)} * inputs_{(j)})$$

Note: β = Outputs. from.hidden–layer

Equation 5

The second hidden layer has also weights, so we have to create an array to store them.

$$\phi_{(ij)} = (weight_{i1}, weights_{i2}, .., weight_{in})$$

φ = second .hidden–layer.weights

Equation 6

Next, we calculate the net input for the second hidden layer:

$$2hlNetInput_{(i)} = \sum_{j=1}^{n} \phi_{(ij)} * Netinputs_{(j)}$$

Equation 7

In order to get the output of the second hidden layer, we have to calculate the following:

$Output2HL_{(i)}$ = Activation Function#2($2hlNetInput_{(i)}$)

If our second hidden layer uses the sigmoid function as its activation function, the equation will be the following:

$$\beta_{(i)} = Sigmoid(\sum_{j=1}^{n} \phi_{(ij)} * Netinputs_{(j)})$$

Note: φ = Outputs. from.second .hidden–layer

Equation 8

The output layer also has weights, so we have to create an array to store them.

$$\delta_{(ij)} = (weight_{i1}, weight_{i2},.., weight_{in})$$

$$\delta = weights.\,from.output{-}layer$$

Equation 9

The net value of the output layer will be calculated in the following way:

$$Net\_values_{(i)} = \sum_{j=1}^{n} \beta_{(ij)} * \delta_{(i)}$$

Equation 10

The last step is to get the 4LBPN output:

$$4LBPNOutput_{(i)} = \text{Output Function}(Net\_values_{(i)})$$

If we use the sigmoid function to do it, we will have the following:

$$4LBPNOutput_{(i)} = Sigmoid(\sum_{j=1}^{n} \beta_{(ij)} * \delta_{(j)})$$

Back Propagation

Equation 11

To measure the net error,

$$\varepsilon_{(n)} = \text{Expected Output}_{(n)} - \text{Net output}_{(n)}$$

or we can use the Generalized Delta Rule:

$$\varepsilon_{(i)} = (\text{Expected Output}_{(i)} - \text{Net output}_{(i)}) * \text{Net output}_{(i)} * (1 - \text{Net output}_{(i)}).$$

Equation 12

To train the net, we update the weights, using an iterative process until the error is minimum.

$$Current\ \alpha_{(ij)} = Previous\ \alpha_{(ij)}\ {}^{*}\varepsilon_{(i)}$$

$$Current\ \varphi_{(ij)} = Previous\ \varphi_{(ij)}\ {}^{*}\varepsilon_{(i)}$$

$$Current\ \delta_{(ij)} = Previous\ \delta_{(ij)}\ {}^{*}\varepsilon_{(i)}$$

When we finish this iteration, the net is trained, so all we have to do is to enter a sample pattern and perform a forward propagation to see if the net recognizes it or not.

PHL: Networks with parallel hidden layers

In this type of network, there are one or more hidden layers in parallel. Each one may contain a different activation function.

As an example, we can think of a network with two hidden layers, each one with a different activation function, both contributing to the network output. The following table illustrates this architecture.

Basic Scheme of a network with parallel hidden layers

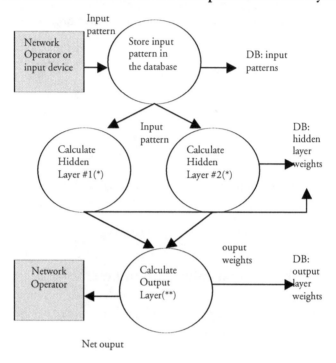

(*) Hidden layer #1=
      activation function #1 (input pattern * weights #1)
      Hidden layer #2=
      activation function #2 (input pattern * weights #2)
(**) Output layer =
      activation function #3 (hidden layer values * output weights)

#1 represents the input layer, which receives the input data. #2 and #3 are the hidden layers in parallel. Each one has its own weights and activation function. The sum of all hidden layers is the input for the output layer.

SOMN: Self Organizing Map Networks
(KOHONEN Network and similar ones)

The group of mapping networks is able to calculate some functional relationship among inputs and outputs. For example, if we use the variable "x" to store the input values, the net could calculate the hyperbolic tangent *tanh("x")* as a standard output.

Characteristic of this network:

- It uses many of the concepts we have seen in the BPN.
- It has two layers: the input-layer and a bidimensional output-layer.
- Each element of the input-layer is associated with an element of the output-layer.
- It uses forward propagation.
- The output-layer units are connected among them. This is called **lateral interaction**.

The lateral interaction emulates the way the neurons work in the neural cortex. When we excite a neuron, we automatically create a positive feedback that excites the neurons that are near it. This excitation is directly proportional to the distance towards the original neuron. We will call this neuron the *winner neuron*.

The Kohonen network is particularly useful for grouping data in categories or classes. Each category then corresponds to an element of the output-layer. The following scheme shows a operational diagram of this network.

Basic Scheme of a Self Organizing Map Network

The classic examples where this architecture is useful are the problems where we need to find a match or nexus among the patterns (for example, if you know the symptoms of a disease and you want to know the name of the pathology).

Self Organizing Map Network

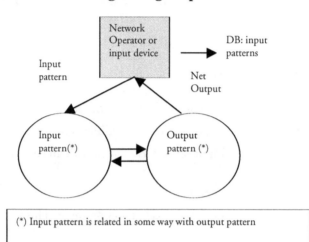

(*) Input pattern is related in some way with output pattern

SOM: How does it work?

We start with an input pattern that will be stored in the input-layer, just as with the BPN.

$$Inputs(i) = (input_{i1}, input_{i2}, ..., input_{in})$$

We also have weights here:

$$Weights(ij) = (weight_{i1}, weights_{i2}, .., weight_{in})$$

We start with random values for the weights.

SOM: Forward Propagation

First, we must calculate the net input of the input-layer

$$NetInput(i) = \sum_{j=1}^{n} weights(ij) * inputs(j)$$

Next, we have to activate the elements of the output-layer

$$Output_{(i)} = NetInput_{(i)} + lateral\ interactions_{(ij)}$$

SOM: Learning algorithm

Our learning algorithm will update the weights using this formula:

New weight$_{(i)}$ = Old weight$_{(i)}$ - (input-Old weight$_{(i)}$)

However, we will only update the weights that are > 0, so we will need an activation function that could help us to do it. We'll use here the *Only-positive()* function, shown in the item "*usual activation functions*" of the BPN section. This function returns 0 if the result is 0 or less than 0. Otherwise, it returns 1. So, our updated weights will be the following:

New weight$_{(i)}$ = Only-positive(New weight$_{(i)}$) * New weight$_{(i)}$

In a SOM, we have to update the connections of the units that are near the winner. In order to calculate the lateral interactions, we start choosing the winner neuron, which is the one that minimizes the difference (in absolute value) between the input array and the weights.

$$winner(i) = Min(\|inputs - weights_i\|)$$

After that, we have to define the "neighborhood" to see which nodes are near the winner. We have already said that all these units have to participate in the learning process. In order to achieve this, we have to define a function to calculate whether a node is near the winner or not. This specific function may vary from application to application. The general rule, however, is that its position in the array (in terms of Row and Column) must be equal to the position of the winner plus/minus a distance (in units), which is set up by the network administrator.

So, our equations to measure proximity are:

$$Row = Winner's\ Row \pm \delta$$

$$Column = Winner's\ Column \pm \delta$$

(Where δ means an arbitrary distance [in units] that was set up by the network administrator.)

So, in other words, the unit "i" will be updated only if $Unit_{(i)}$ is near Winner(i).

During the training process, the weights have to be updated in an iterative process until the net outputs become stable and the net calculates just one winner for each pattern loaded.

SOM: Mathematical equations

We start with an array for the inputs and one for the weights:

Equation 1

$$Inputs(i) = (input_{i1}, input_{i2}, ..., input_{in})$$

Equation 2

$$Weights(ij) = (weight_{i1}, weights_{i2}, ..., weight_{in})$$

Forward propagation

To calculate the value for each unit of the output-layer, we will have the following:

Equation 3

$$diff\,(i) = \sqrt{\sum_{j=1}^{i}(inputs(j) - weights(ij))2}$$

*Where I is the length of the inputs array

Next, we have to calculate the winner. The winner unit is the one that minimizes the difference between inputs and weights. So, in other words, is the minimum $diff_{(i)}$

Equation 4

Winner(i) = $\textbf{\textit{Min}}(diff_{(i)})$

Now we have to see which units are near the winner.

This ASP function checks if a unit is near the winner. The distance must be set up by the network operator.

```
Function near(row,col,winner_row, winner_col,distance)
near = false
row = sqrt((winner_row - row)^2)//This gives us the absolute value from
the equation
column = sqrt((winner_col - col)^2)
If row <= distance and column <= distance then
near = true
end if
end function
```

Propagating Lateral intersections

Equation 5

Once we have found the winner, and we can calculate the distance among units, we have to propagate the lateral intersections. We use the Only-positive() function (shown in the section related to activation functions of the BPN) to be sure that only the positive weights will be uploaded.

Current Weight$_{(i)}$ = (Previous Weight(i) + (Input(i) - Previous Weight(i))   {unit i is near the winner

Current Weight$_{(i)}$ = Only-positive(Current Weight(i))   {update only if it is positive

In order to train all the units of the net, we have to create a function that:

a) Calculates the winner

b) Checks if all the other units are near the winner

c) Updates the weights if point b) is true

d) Loops until the net is stable

SAM: Self Associative Memory Networks (SAM)

This type of network consists of two layers, the input layer and the output layer, but in some way, both of them are the same.

This network is similar to the previous one, but has an outstanding advantage: The input layer is a defective entrance of a pattern and the network tries to return the complete or non-defective pattern.

For example: If we look for "John Doe" but by mistake we enter "John Due," a SAM will give back "John Doe." A SAM network associated to a telephone directory makes it possible to write an incorrect name and retrieve back the correct addresses of all the people whose names are similar.

SAM answers the following question: *What are the names in the database that are similar to the one I am entering?* If we just talk about text, there are also generic algorithms that perform a similar task. The network, however, can do the same with any pattern. Therefore the recognition is not limited to text. In other words: We can input a digital X-ray pattern with a fracture in a bone and ask the network to find all similar cases stored in the database. Table A5.8 shows the basic scheme of a SAM.

Example:

We have previously used an example where we wanted to recognize the pattern of the number "1." In other words: we want to recognize the shape#1

Shape 1

1

When we digitalize the pattern, the computer recognizes a pixels grid such as Shape#2:

Shape 2

```
0 0 1 0 0
0 1 1 0 0
0 0 1 0 0
0 0 1 0 0
0 1 1 1 0
```

But now: What happens if the input pattern is Shape#3? We can recognize that it is a defective copy of the Shape#2. The idea is that the computer could be able to do the same.

Shape 3

```
0 0 1 0 0
0 1 0 0 0
0 0 1 0 0
0 0 1 0 0
0 1 1 0 0
```

Given a defective input such as Shape#3, SAM should be able to match it to the correct shape (in this case, shape#2). Therefore, it is expected that the net could identify Shape#3 as the number "1."

This is extremely useful to recognize, for example, text from a dusty Xerox machine copy, or a scratched piece of paper. When we talked about OCR (Optical Character Recognition), we said that the traditional algorithmic methods fail when we are in the presence of a defective piece of paper or a Xerox copy.

TABLE A5.8

Basic Scheme of a Self Associative Memory Network

I	Input	Output	O
N	Layer	Layer	U
P	contains	returns	T
U	a	the	P
T	defective	correct	U
S	pattern	pattern	T
			S

$\rightarrow$

```
P W
A R
T O
T N
E G
R
N

1
```

$\rightarrow$

$\leftarrow$

```
P O
A K
T
T
E
R
N

1
```

$\rightarrow$

Self Associative Memory Network

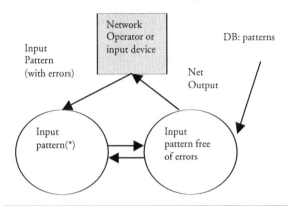

(*) The output pattern is the input pattern free of errors. The net returns the correct version of the input pattern

SAM: Structure

It is a network composed of two layers: an input and an output layer. We do not have to train the net, just calculate the weights initially. Once we have done it, we can enter a pattern similar to the original and the net will recover the first original one. This is useful when we are working with damaged patterns and we want to recover the original information.

$$Inputs(i) = (input_{i1}, input_{i2}, ..., input_{in})$$

$$Outputs(i) = (output_{i1}, output_{i2}, ..., output_{in})$$

We will call them just α and β, so our arrays will be:

$$\alpha_{(i)} = Inputs(i)$$

$$\beta_{(i)} = Outputs(i)$$

In this kind of network we use the [1, -1] format for the patterns, also called bipolar notation. Thus, we will get the following:

$$\exists \alpha_{(i)} / \alpha_{(i)} \in \Re \wedge (\alpha_{(i)} = \pm 1)$$

$$\exists \beta_{(i)} / \beta_{\omega i)} \in \Re \wedge (\beta_{(i)} = \pm 1)$$

Here there is only one array for the weights. We calculate the weights multiplying the input array α by the output array β.

$$weights_{(ij)} = \sum_{j=1}^{n} \alpha_{(ij)} * \beta_{(j)}$$

$$weights_{(i,j)} = (\alpha_1 * \beta_1, \alpha_2 * \beta_1, \alpha_3 * \beta_1, \ldots \alpha_{in} * \beta_{jn})$$

Once we have calculated our weights, the net is ready.

When using it, the net operator enters a new pattern. As we have previously discussed, there must be a damaged copy of the original input pattern, so as the net tries to recognize it. In our example, the original pattern is stored in the array α. The operator enters a new set of data. We will allocate it in an array called δ.

$$\delta_{(i)} = (\delta_{i1}, \delta_{i2}, \ldots, \delta_{in})$$

$\delta_{(i)}$ is a copy of $\alpha_{(i)}$ with noise (a defective copy), so both of them will have the same length.

At this moment, we have four elements:

$\alpha_{(i)}$: Contains the original pattern
$\beta_{(i)}$: Contains the original outputs
$Weights_{(ij)}$: Contains the weights
$\delta_{(i)}$: Contains our sample pattern. SAM will try to recognize it.

SAM will try to determinate if $\delta_{(i)}$ is a copy of $\alpha_{(i)}$, even if $\delta_{(i)}$ is damaged. If it succeeds, it will return the correct pattern $\alpha_{(i)}$ as an output.

Though we can think there is a forward and a back propagation process here, it is better to think in a continuous circular forward propagation where the input $\delta_{(i)}$ propagates and gets $\beta_{(i)}$ that propagates in the opposite direction and returns $\delta_{(i+1)}$. As $\delta_{(i+1)}$ must have bipolar values (-1 or 1), we have to use an output function to turn them into the proper format. When we talked about Back-Prop Networks, we saw a function called *Dec2Bip()* that was used to turn any number into 1 or -1. This function is simple: It returns -1 if the input is 0.5 or less. Otherwise, it returns 1. In a SAM environment, we use this function as the standard output function. If $\delta_{(i+1)}$ is equal to $\alpha_{(i)}$, the net returns a message informing the human operator about this fact, and the execution finishes. Otherwise, the net propagates $\delta_{(i+1)}$. This iteration continues until a match is found or the net determines that the patterns are different. This process can be seen in the following diagram:

Sequence of SAM

$$\delta_{(i)} \rightarrow \beta_{(i)} \rightarrow \delta_{(i+1)} \begin{cases} = \alpha_{(i)} & \text{Match} \\ \text{Not==} \ \alpha_{(i)} & \text{Iterate using } \delta_{(i+1)} \text{ as the new } \delta_{(i)} \ (*) \end{cases}$$

(*) This iteration process continues until the patterns match or SAM recognizes that there is no match among them.

In the Web page for this book you can see SAM working. Feel free to download the source code if you are interested in it. You may use the password "1949" to enter:

http://www5.domaindlx.com/mgbosq/nnets.html

If you cannot enter to the site you can write the author at mgbosq@sinectis.com.ar and ask him for an alternative way to get the code.

Mathematical Equations of a SAM

First of all, we have to load the inputs and outputs in two arrays:

Equation 1

$$\alpha_{(i)} = \textit{Inputs}(i)$$

$$\beta_{(i)} = \textit{Outputs}(i)$$

Equation 2

Both α and β values must be 1 or -1

$$\exists \alpha_{(i)}/\alpha_{(i)} \in \Re \wedge (\alpha_{(i)} = \pm 1)$$

$$\exists \beta_{(i)}/\beta_{\omega i)} \in \Re \wedge (\beta_{(i)} = \pm 1)$$

Equation 3

The weights must be calculated multiplying these arrays

$$weights_{(ij)} = \sum_{j=1}^{n} \alpha_{(ij)} * \beta_{(j)}$$

Forward Propagation

Equation 4

Now we have to load our sample pattern.

$$\delta_{(i)} = (\delta_{i1}, \delta_{i2}, \ldots, \delta_{in})$$

Equation 5

We calculate the new $\beta(i)$ values

$$\beta_{(i)} = \sum_{j=1}^{n} weights_{(ij)} * \phi_{(j)}$$

Equation 6

We use Dec2bip() as the output

Jump Connection Networks

It is similar to a BPN, the difference being that each layer is connected to all the other layers.

In the following diagram each circle represents a layer of the network and the arrows represent the connections. We see that each new layer receives connections of all the previous layers; that is the reason why the training and the execution of the network is slower than a BPN. The more layers it has, the slower it trains.

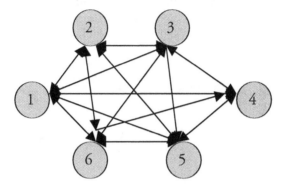

In this example, layer 1 is the input layer, layer 4 is the output layer, and the others are the hidden layers.

SUMMARY

Here there is a short summary of the steps needed to design an Artificial Neural Network:

Step 1: Capture digitalized data:

In order to enter data into the N-Net, we will need to use some kind of device.

Frequent Devices used to Capture Data

- Human operator
- Internet Connection
- E-mail
- Digital camera
- Video camera
- Scanner
- Digital prints reader
- Sound recorder/microphone
- Web-cam

Step 2: Generate memory spaces. This can be done by the creation of multiple memory arrays.

One of the ways to artificially simulate neurons is to assimilate them to elements of arrays or vectors. Any programming language offers the possibility of creating n-dimensional arrays. The amount of arrays depends on the architecture of the network to choose. The selection of the ideal architecture requires a detailed analysis that exceeds the capacity of these pages. This work has been made thinking about the architecture of a Backward propagation Network or BPN with one hidden layer.

The initial number of arrays involved will be the following:

I) One array to store the input layer whose number of elements agrees with the number of elements of this layer.

II) One array to store the hidden layer of variable size (with the same size of the input layer).

III) One array to store the output layer with a variable number of elements according to the number of outputs that must have the network.

In this step the arrays are usually filled with null values, generally zeros.

<u>Step 3: Set an order of preference or "weight" to the layers, symbolizing in this way the different strengths among layers and neurons</u>

As has been explained in preceding paragraphs, the network tries to simulate the energy movement in the synaptic interconnection, reinforcing the frequent connections.

This is obtained by annexing to each value of the layer a random value called **weight** in the specific vocabulary. The weights are then values, which are multiplied by the new values of the layers to obtain the outputs or results that are transferred from one layer to the following one.

The function of the weights is to recognize and separate one pattern from another. **Before executing the net, the weights must be configured in a process called "training."**

In other words: Once the network software has been developed, and before the N-net is ready to work, the operator must "train" the software to make it recognize the patterns. **A neural network is a form of software that learns, but this learning must be done before the execution.** Once the network is trained, a new set of weights are made, which can be saved in a database. When the network is required to work, it only has to call those values saved in the database and load them as weights values.

The network will then need the following:

IV) One array to store the input-layer weights.

This array will have the same number of elements as the input layer and will have also stored the relative strengths to each pattern that the network can recognize That is the reason why it must be a two-dimension array.

Example:

If the input layer has 1000 elements and the network can recognize 8 different patterns, the array will have one first dimension of 1000 and one second dimension of 8. To program this array in a computer, in ASP, we should write the following: DIM WEIGHTS (1000,8)

VI) One array to store the hidden layer weights

This array must contain at least the same elements as the output array

<u>Step 4: Assign to the first array the status of input layer, which will contain the digital data.</u>

As has been said before, the values taken from a capture device are supposed to be placed in a database. These values must be turned into a binary string, and entered in the "input layer" array.

The network can load the initial data from just a database or a combined set of a data-entry device and a database. The first option means that there are some external input devices that capture the patterns and enter them into a database, which is used by the network to input the data.

In the second option, if the data-entry device is integrated to the neural network, it can capture the input layer data and enter it into the net, so the input database is just necessary to store the weights and the output data.

Step 5: Assign to the last array the status of output layer, allowing that its values could be transformed by the interaction of the other elements of the network.

If the network has already been trained and configured, there must be a database with the output values previously entered. It is in this moment when the output layer array is loaded with the output values taken from the database.

Step 6: Assign to the intermediate layers the status of hidden layers, allowing that their values could be modified by the interaction of the other elements of the network.

The values of the hidden layers will be transformed by the interaction of the other elements of the net. This process must be repeated for all the hidden layers. In the default example in this book, there is a one hidden-layer network, so we'll have just one hidden layer. Nevertheless, other architectures may use two or more hidden layers.

Step 7: Forward Propagate: To make operations of transference among the data of the layers, simulating in this way the synaptic interconnections.

Forward & Back Propagation

Forward propagation is a way used to simulate the synaptic interconnection process. The data are transferred from one array to the next one, simulating the neural flow of electric impulses. This transference is called "propagation." In the case of forward propagation the flow follows the natural order, from the input layer to the output layer. The opposite is the back-propagation, where the data flows from the output layer to the input layer.

In the forward propagation, once we have entered the pattern in the input layer and its weights, the net calculates the hidden layer values for that input layer. With those values of the hidden layer, and having the weights for the hidden layer, the net then calculates the output layer values for that input pattern and loads them in the "output layer" array of the network.

In summary: Propagation starts with the input layer value and calculates the outputs for those patterns.

Step 8: Get the output layer values, which will be taken as the network value for a given input value.

This value will be the result of the net search. The value can be stored in a memory variable or saved in a database field for later use. Some nets convert the result to another format before saving it, because the raw result is generally a number. If the net uses a database with these numbers associated with proper descriptions, then the final answer could be a description instead of a number.

Step 9: Set up the actions attached to the network output: (Ex: The creation of an information file, or the activation of an automatic robotic device)

The network output can be attached to another computer program. This second program could be executed once the net reaches its answer.

In this case, the net commands the way the program is executed and sets up the behavior of the second program.

CHAPTER 3

How to Input Data into the Neural Network

I consider this to be an important chapter. Most of the books about Neural Networks do not make any reference to the input of data in the net. They only mention a few words about it. I am not surprised that many of the frequent questions that I receive are related to this process. That is the reason why I have decided to include a chapter referring to said subject in this book.

First of all: I do not know how much you know about digital data, so I will explain some basic principles. You may start reading the chapter, and if you sense you already know the first part of it, just skip up to its main section, called "Working with patterns stored in graphic files."

Digital images: Basic principles

Computers use the binary system for image representation, which admits only values of 0 and 1.

In order to put information into this system, there is a technique that consists of transforming any information into a string of zeros and ones.

The information exists in different formats:

- Numbers
- Letters
- Computer characters as the sign "?"

- Photographs
- Drawings in a piece of paper
- X-rays
- Musical tunes
- Radar signals
- Radio signals
- TV signals
- Computed Topography

Case I: Numbers

If the information is numerical, it is enough to turn the number into $base_2$ (binary).

Let us remember that ordinary numbers are expressed in $base_{10}$, nomenclature that means the following:

1234 in $base_{10}$ means that said number comes from the sum of:

$4 \times 10^0 = 4$
$+3 \times 10^1 = 30$
$+2 \times 10^2 = 200$
$+1 \times 10^3 = 1000$

$\overline{1000 + 200 + 30 + 4 = 1234}$

1001 in $base_2$ means that it comes from the sum of:

$+1 \times 2^0 = 1$
$+0 \times 2^1 = 0$
$+0 \times 2^2 = 0$
$+1 \times 2^3 = 8$

$\overline{1 + 0 + 0 + 8 = 9}$

In other words, 1001 in $base_2$ is equal to 9 in $base_{10}$.

Every number expressed in $base_2$ has its equivalent in $base_{10}$ and vice-versa.

Cases 2, 3: Letters, characters

There are ways to transform letters into numbers and vice-versa. One of the best known codes is the ASCII code. It consists of 255 characters corresponding to all the numbers, the letters, and the common characters used in computers.

Any letter can be turned into a number using this code, and the last numbers can be digitalized using the procedure shown in the previous step.

Cases 4-6: Photographs, drawings & X-rays

Scanners are devices that digitalize photos, drawings, or X-rays. They divide the photo into thousands of tiny points called pixels. A photograph consists of the sum of pixels that it contains.

A number is assigned to each pixel, corresponding to a predefined color scale. We then have a string of numbers that operate via the procedure shown in case 1.

The usual color scales have 16 colors, 256 colors, or 16 million colors. The size of the arizing string is proportional to the number of colors used. This string is recorded in a computer file and works as shown in case 1. This point is so important that we will continue talking about it throughout this chapter.

Cases 7-12: Musical tunes, Radars, Sonar, Radio Signals

Digital sound recorders divide the sound melody into small waves that are impossible for human beings to hear. Then a standard code number is assigned to them.

The MIDI code is the most popular one for digital music at the moment. The sound is converted into a string of numbers, which is managed according to the procedure shown in step 1.

Digital reproducers use this string as input, and decode the string to reproduce the equivalent sound of each stored number.

In the case of a radar or a sonar signal, the bounce of the emitted wave is caught by ad-hoc devices. The treatment is similar to that of a sound wave.

Generation of input layers

The neural network must start with an artificial stimulus to be able to operate. In a living organism the stimulation is achieved by the excitation of any of the senses or a combination of several.

In a computer, this process must be divided in two parts:

1. The opening of the neural network program, which requires external human activation to work. This is an automatic task in living beings.
2. The requirement of an input (a pattern to be recognized).

Any input must be turned into a digital format to be transformed into a file that is able to be understood by the computer.

To digitalize information we must transform the input data into a zero-one string, which is called a "binary string." This string must be stored in a file or database that keeps the information. In general, we can use a vector or an array to increase the speed of the process. (An array locates the patterns in RAM, so the data search is faster than a database location.) As we have already seen, the data is grouped into "layers" in the net, so we can say that the input pattern can be considered as the input layer. That is the reason why the vector is named "**Input Layer.**"

Example of an Input layer

Let's suppose that we want to make an OCR Neural Network. Let us suppose we have a scanner that digitalizes some textbooks. What we need is a net that could be able to recognize the patterns and turn them into letters and numbers to be placed in a database. The scanner reads the piece of paper and generates a graphic file as a result of such a process. (A .GIF or .JPG graphic file containing a shape that represents a letter or a number.) Suppose we place in the scanner a piece of paper with just this shape:

Shape 1

1

A human being (at this point we can speak of a *carbon neural network*) recognizes in less than a second that this is number one. The computer just sees a symbol. Remember that we have NOT pressed the "1" key in the keyboard. The machine only has a graphic file with a shape in it. The goal is to make the computer recognize it as the number one.

The composition of a graphic file is a series of dark dots and white dots. When the dots are put close together, they simulate solid shapes. We will use the term pixels for the dots. Each pixel has a color attached to it. Therefore, we can say that the graphic file is a string of white and black pixels. The "noise" in the scanned pieces of paper is due to a scanning error whereby a white pixel is seen as a black one.

If we separate the pixels from the file a bit, the shape would look like this:

Shape 2

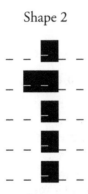

Shape 2 is the same image as Shape 1. The only difference is that the pixels have been separated a bit to show each one by itself.

In order to work with a neural network, the graphic file must be converted into a binary string.

To complete it, the white pixels must be replaced by a "0" and each black string can be replaced by a "1." So our shape becomes like this one:

Shape 3

0 0 1 0 0
0 1 1 0 0
0 0 1 0 0
0 0 1 0 0
0 0 1 0 0

If we show the same data in a binary string format, (Row1 + Row2 + Row3, etc.) we will have the following one:

String 1

0 0 1 0 0 0 1 1 0 0 0 0 1 0 0 0 0 1 0 0 0 0 1 0 0

String1 is now a suitable data format to establish the input for the net. We will call it a "pattern," so the input pattern for Shape 1 (the initial shape) is the following:

Input Pattern 1 (0-1 format)

0, 0, 1, 0, 0, 0, 1, 1, 0, 0, 0, 0 1, 0, 0, 0, 0, 1, 0, 0, 0, 0, 1, 0, 0

Proper Formats for the Patterns

Some authors recommend storing the patterns using values from 0.1 to 0.9 instead of 0 to 1. The reason is simple: When you multiply by 0, the result is 0, so the net requires more time to be trained.

I personally sometimes use 0.01-0.99 with the same effect. So, one of the things that a Neural Network developer has to think of is the data format he will use in the net.

Our input pattern could then be the following one:

Input Pattern 1 (0.1-0.9 format)

> 0.1, 0.1, **0.9**, 0.1, 0.1, 0.1, **0.9**, **0.9**, 0.1, 0.1, 0.1, 0.1, **0.9**,
> 0.1, 0.1, 0.1, 0.1, **0.9**, 0.1, 0.1, 0.1, **0.9**, **0.9**, **0.9**, 0.1

Nevertheless, it could also be like this one:

Input Pattern 1 (0.01-0.99 format)

> 0.01, 0.01, **0.99**, 0.01, 0.01, 0.01, **0.99**, **0.99**, 0.01, 0.01,
> 0.01, 0.01, **0.99**, 0.01, 0.01, 0.01, 0.01, **0.99**, 0.01, 0.01,
> 0.01, **0.99**, **0.99**, **0.99**, 0.01

or like this one:

Input Pattern 1 (1-1 format)

> -1, -1, **1**, -1, -1, -1, **1**, **1**, -1, -1,-1, -1 **1**, -1, -1,-1,-1, **1**, -1, -1,
> -1, **1**, **1**, **1**, -1

Working with Patterns Stored in Text Files

This part of the chapter takes us closer to reality.

The easiest way to start working is to create our patterns in a text file. We can use any word processor for this. All you have to do is create a matrix and fill it with a specific character. In general the asterisk (*) is a good character to work with.

Here is a series of four patterns made with a word processor. These examples are included in the web page of this book for readers to play with. This series is called "SHAPES."

"SHAPES" series of patterns

PATTERN 1	PATTERN2	PATTERN 3	PATTERN 4
Circle	Square	Parallel lines	X
* *	* * * *		
* *	* *		* *
* *	* *	* * * *	*
* *	* * * *	* * * *	* *

That is all you have to do. Easy, isn't it? If we work with text files we can now jump to the section named "Converting an Image into an Input Pattern," which can be found at the end of this chapter.

Working with Patterns Stored in Graphic Files

First of all: Neural Networks are not able to make any difference among colors, so it is easier if we work with Black & White images.

In general, patterns will come to us in a multimedia file. If it is a visual pattern, it may come in a standard image format as .jpg, .gif, .tiff, .bmp, or .eps. If we use a digital camera to take digital photographs of the patterns, the image will generally be a .jpg. All the photo editors (such as Microsoft Photo editor, or Microsoft Paint, which are included in the Windows installation CD-ROM) let us interchange the formats. Thus, if we have a .jpg image, we can turn it into other formats. There are two such formats that are useful for Neural Nets Inputs. One of them is the .bmp format. It creates "bitmaps" which are exact representations of the shapes. This characteristic makes them easy to work with. So, our first step with a digital image is to turn it into a .bmp format. Here we will see how to use a .bmp file as an input pattern for the net:

Let us start with these images:

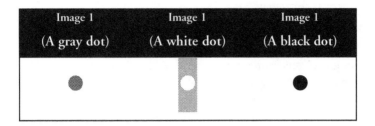

They are placed in three .bmp files: dot1.bmp, dot2.bmp, dot3.bmp.

Now we will rename the .bmp files as .txt, so we will have the following files: dot1.txt, dot2.txt, and dot3.txt.

Next, we have to open the files with any text editor, such as "WordPad" (which is included in the Windows installation program).

What we will see is the following:

File: Gray Circle—dot1.txt from dot1.bmp. Raw Sample

```
BM6 6 ( • • • )
ÿÿÿÿÿÿÿÿÿÿÿÿÿÿÿÿÿÿÿÿÿÿÿÿÿÿÿÿÿÿÿÿÿÿÿÿÿÿÿÿÿÿÿÿÿÿÿÿÿÿÿÿÿÿÿÿÿÿÿÿ
ÿÿÿÿÿÿÿÿÿÿÿÿÿÿÿÿÿÿÿÿÿÿÿÿÿÿÿÿÿÿÿÿÿÿÿÿÿÿÿÿÿÿÿÿÿÿÿÿÿÿÿÿÿÿÿÿÿÿÿÿ
ÿÿÿÿÿÿÿÿÿÿÿÿÿÿÿÿÿÿÿÿÿÿÿÿÿÿÿÿÿÿÿÿÿÿÿÿÿÿÿÿÿÿÿÿÿÿÿÿÿÿÿÿÿÿÿÿÿÿÿÿ
ÿÿÿÿÿÿÿÿÿÿÿÿÿÿÿÿÿÿÿÿÿÿÿÿÿÿÿÿÿÿÿÿÿÿÿÿÿÿÿÿÿÿÿÿÿÿÿÿÿÿÿÿÿÿÿÿÿÿÿÿ
ÿÿÿÿÿÿÿÿÿÿÿÿÿÿÿÿÿÿÿÿÿÿÿÿÿÿÿÿâââââââââââââââââââÿÿÿÿÿÿÿÿÿÿÿÿÿ
ÿÿÿÿÿÿÿÿÿÿÿÿÿÿÿÿÿâââââââââââââââââââââââÿÿÿÿÿÿÿÿÿÿÿÿÿÿÿÿÿÿÿÿ
ÿÿÿÿâââââââââââââââââââââââââââââÿÿÿÿÿÿÿÿÿÿÿÿÿÿÿÿÿÿÿâââââââ
âââââââââââââââââââââââââââââÿÿÿÿÿÿÿÿÿÿÿÿÿÿâââââââââââââââââ
âââââââââââââââââÿÿÿÿÿÿÿÿÿÿÿÿÿÿÿââââââââââââââââââââââââââââ
âââââââââÿÿÿÿÿÿÿÿÿÿÿÿÿÿââââââââââââââââââââââââââââââââââââ
ÿÿÿÿÿÿÿÿÿÿÿÿÿÿâââââââââââââââââââââââââââââââââââÿÿÿÿÿÿÿÿÿÿÿ
ÿÿÿâââââââââââââââââââââââââââââââââââââÿÿÿÿÿÿÿÿÿÿÿÿÿÿÿÿÿâââ
ââââââââââââââââââââââââÿÿÿÿÿÿÿÿÿÿÿÿÿÿÿÿÿÿÿÿââââââââââââââ
ââââââââââÿÿÿÿÿÿÿÿÿÿÿÿÿÿÿÿÿÿÿÿÿÿÿÿÿÿÿÿÿÿâââââââââââââââââÿÿ
ÿÿÿÿÿÿÿÿÿÿÿÿÿÿÿÿÿÿÿÿÿÿÿÿÿÿÿÿÿÿÿÿÿÿÿÿÿÿÿÿÿÿÿÿÿÿÿÿÿÿÿÿÿÿÿÿÿÿÿÿ
ÿÿÿÿÿÿÿÿÿÿÿÿÿÿÿÿÿÿÿÿÿÿÿÿÿÿÿÿÿÿÿÿÿÿÿÿÿÿÿÿÿÿÿÿÿÿÿÿÿÿÿÿÿÿÿÿÿÿÿÿ
ÿÿÿÿÿÿÿÿÿÿÿÿÿÿÿÿÿÿÿÿÿÿÿÿÿÿÿÿÿÿÿÿÿÿÿÿÿÿÿÿÿÿÿÿÿÿÿÿÿÿÿÿÿÿÿÿÿÿÿÿ
ÿÿÿÿÿÿÿÿÿÿÿÿÿÿÿÿÿÿÿÿ
```

The first row is the file header. It is not important at all. We will not pay attention to it.

The following rows trace a map (a bitmap) of the shape. We have to observe that the file has more or less a square form. Blank spaces are represented by the ÿ character, and gray dots are represented by the â character. Next, we have to place a paragraph mark (generally an ENTER mark) every 50 characters. In other words, we will create a table with 50 columns and several rows. What we get is the following:

File: Gray Circle—dot1.txt from dot1.bmp

```
ÿÿÿÿÿÿÿÿÿÿÿÿÿÿÿÿÿÿÿÿÿÿÿÿÿÿÿÿÿÿÿÿÿÿÿÿÿÿÿÿÿÿÿÿÿÿÿÿÿÿ
ÿÿÿÿÿÿÿÿÿÿÿÿÿÿÿÿÿÿÿÿÿÿÿÿÿÿÿÿÿÿÿÿÿÿÿÿÿÿÿÿÿÿÿÿÿÿÿÿÿÿ
ÿÿÿÿÿÿÿÿÿÿÿÿÿÿÿÿÿÿÿÿÿÿÿÿÿÿÿÿÿÿÿÿÿÿÿÿÿÿÿÿÿÿÿÿÿÿÿÿÿÿ
ÿÿÿÿÿÿÿÿÿÿÿÿÿÿÿÿÿÿÿÿÿÿÿÿÿÿÿÿÿÿÿÿÿÿÿÿÿÿÿÿÿÿÿÿÿÿÿÿÿÿ
ÿÿÿÿÿÿÿÿÿÿÿÿÿÿÿÿÿÿÿÿÿÿÿÿÿÿÿÿÿÿÿÿÿÿÿÿÿÿÿÿÿÿÿÿÿÿÿÿÿÿ
ÿÿÿÿÿÿÿÿÿÿÿÿÿÿÿÿâââââââââââââââââââÿÿÿÿÿÿÿÿÿÿÿÿÿÿÿÿ
ÿÿÿÿÿÿÿÿÿÿÿÿÿÿâââââââââââââââââââââÿÿÿÿÿÿÿÿÿÿÿÿÿÿÿ
ÿÿÿÿÿÿÿÿÿÿÿâââââââââââââââââââââââââââÿÿÿÿÿÿÿÿÿÿÿ
ÿÿÿÿÿÿÿÿâââââââââââââââââââââââââââââââÿÿÿÿÿÿÿÿ
ÿÿÿÿÿÿÿâââââââââââââââââââââââââââââââââÿÿÿÿÿÿÿ
ÿÿÿÿÿÿÿâââââââââââââââââââââââââââââââââÿÿÿÿÿÿÿ
ÿÿÿÿÿÿÿâââââââââââââââââââââââââââââââââÿÿÿÿÿÿÿ
ÿÿÿÿÿÿÿâââââââââââââââââââââââââââââââââÿÿÿÿÿÿÿ
ÿÿÿÿÿÿÿâââââââââââââââââââââââââââââââââÿÿÿÿÿÿÿ
ÿÿÿÿÿÿÿÿâââââââââââââââââââââââââââââââÿÿÿÿÿÿÿÿ
ÿÿÿÿÿÿÿÿÿÿÿâââââââââââââââââââââââââââÿÿÿÿÿÿÿÿÿÿÿ
ÿÿÿÿÿÿÿÿÿÿÿÿÿÿâââââââââââââââââ ÿÿÿÿÿÿÿÿÿÿÿÿÿÿÿ
ÿÿÿÿÿÿÿÿÿÿÿÿÿÿÿÿÿÿÿÿÿÿÿÿÿÿÿÿÿÿÿÿÿÿÿÿÿÿÿÿÿÿÿÿÿÿÿÿÿÿ
ÿÿÿÿÿÿÿÿÿÿÿÿÿÿÿÿÿÿÿÿÿÿÿÿÿÿÿÿÿÿÿÿÿÿÿÿÿÿÿÿÿÿÿÿÿÿÿÿÿÿ
ÿÿÿÿÿÿÿÿÿÿÿÿÿÿÿÿÿÿÿÿÿÿÿÿÿÿÿÿÿÿÿÿÿÿÿÿÿÿÿÿÿÿÿÿÿÿÿÿÿÿ
ÿÿÿÿÿÿÿÿÿÿÿÿÿÿÿÿÿÿÿÿÿÿÿÿÿÿÿÿÿÿÿÿÿÿÿÿÿÿÿÿÿÿÿÿÿÿÿÿÿÿ
```

I have placed the â character in boldface, just to remark it. I will make the following examples more realistic; I will not remark the inner circle.

We can perfectly see the circle made by â characters. This is the beauty of the .bmp format: It creates for us the patterns we need as input layers of the net!

The same happens when we change the colors of the shape. The .bmp format just changes the character, but the pattern of the dot is the same.

There are other formats that work in a similar way. One of them is the .eps format. If we turn the file from .bmp into .eps we will get the following pattern:

File: Gray Circle—dot1.txt from dot1.eps

```
FFFFFFFFFFFFFFFFFFFFFFFFFFFFFFFFFFFFFFFFFFFFFFFFFFFFFFFFFFFFFF
FFFFFFFFFFFFFFFFFFFFFFFFFFFFFFFFFFFFFFFFFFFFFFFFFFFFFFFFFFFFFF
FFFFFFFFFFFFFFFFFFFFFFFFFFFFFFFFFFFFFFFFFFFFFFFFFFFFFFFFFFFFFF
FFFFFFFFFFFFFFFFFFFFFFFFFFFFFFFFFFFFFFFFFFFFFFFFFFFFFFFFFFFFFF
FFFFFFFFFFFFFFFFFFFFFFFFFFFFFFFFFFFFFFFFFFFFFFFFFFFFFFFFFFFFFF
FFFFFFFFFFFFFFFFFFFFFFFFFFFFFFFFFFFFFFFFFFFFFFFFFFFFFFFFFFFFFF
FFFFFFFFFFFFFFFFFFF808080808080808080808080808080FFFFFFFFFFFFFFF
FFFFFFFFFFFF80808080808080808080808080808080808080FFFFFFFFFF
FFFFFF80808080808080808080808080808080808080808080808080FFFFF
FF808080808080808080808080808080808080808080808080808080FF
FF808080808080808080808080808080808080808080808080808080FF
FF808080808080808080808080808080808080808080808080808080FF
FF808080808080808080808080808080808080808080808080808080FF
FF808080808080808080808080808080808080808080808080808080FF
FF808080808080808080808080808080808080808080808080808080FF
FFFFFF80808080808080808080808080808080808080808080808080FFFFF
FFFFFFFFFFFF80808080808080808080808080808080808080FFFFFFFFFF
FFFFFFFFFFFFFFFFFFF808080808080808080808080808080FFFFFFFFFFFFFFF
FFFFFFFFFFFFFFFFFFFFFFFFFFFFFFFFFFFFFFFFFFFFFFFFFFFFFFFFFFFFFF
FFFFFFFFFFFFFFFFFFFFFFFFFFFFFFFFFFFFFFFFFFFFFFFFFFFFFFFFFFFFFF
FFFFFFFFFFFFFFFFFFFFFFFFFFFFFFFFFFFFFFFFFFFFFFFFFFFFFFFFFFFFFF
FFFFFFFFFFFFFFFFFFFFFFFFFFFFFFFFFFFFFFFFFFFFFFFFFFFFFFFFFFFFFF
```

You can notice that the shape is same. The background is now made by the hexa-decimal FF number (255), which represents the white color, and the gray color is represented by the number 80.

Here each row contains 120 characters. Both "FF" and "80" use two characters, so we can deduce that each row represents 120/2 = 60 pixels of the image.

At this point we are able to affirm that formats like .bmp or .eps make a "map" of the shapes. The only difference between the files is the code used by the .bmp to mark the different colors.

Converting the Image into an Input Pattern

In order to create an input pattern, all the patterns have to be transformed into a 0-1 format. All we have to do is to replace â with 0 and ÿ with 1.

The result is the following:

Input layer from file dot1.txt

```
000000000000000000000000000000000000000000000000000
000000000000000000000000000000000000000000000000000
000000000000000000000000000000000000000000000000000
000000000000000000000000000000000000000000000000000
000000000000000000000000000000000000000000000000000
00000000000000011111111111111111110000000000000000
00000000000011111111111111111111111110000000000000
00000000001111111111111111111111111111110000000000
00000001111111111111111111111111111111111110000000
00000001111111111111111111111111111111111110000000
00000001111111111111111111111111111111111110000000
00000001111111111111111111111111111111111110000000
00000001111111111111111111111111111111111110000000
00000001111111111111111111111111111111111110000000
00000000001111111111111111111111111111110000000000
00000000000011111111111111111111111110000000000000
00000000000000011111111111111111110000000000000000
000000000000000000000000000000000000000000000000000
000000000000000000000000000000000000000000000000000
000000000000000000000000000000000000000000000000000
000000000000000000000000000000000000000000000000000
```

Notice that the net will only recognize patterns, not colors. All three patterns will be the same for it. The net cannot distinguish between a red dot and a black one.

Final step: Entering the Input Pattern in the Net

Once we have got the input pattern, we have to store it in the database of the N-Net.

In the example used in this book, I have used a database that has a table to store the input patterns. It can be a SQL or an Access database.

In order to store the input patterns shown in this book, I have used a table with the following structure...

Layer	Row	Column	Value	Comment

...where each column represents...

Layer: We use 1 for the input patterns, and 10 for the expected values (used to train the net)

Row: Represent the number of elements of each pattern

Column: Each pattern has an ID (1,2,3,4, etc.). We place it here

Value: It refers to the value of each element of the pattern

Comment: To make comments about the data stored

Example: Let us suppose we want to work with the following structure. It represents the premises of the logic AND operator:

a) A premise which is the result of a False premise, AND a False premise is False

b) A premise which is the result of a True premise, AND a False premise is False

c) A premise which is the result of a False premise, AND a True premise is False

d) A premise which is the result of a True premise, AND a True premise is True

Finally, we will get the following:

e) False, False is False
f) False, **True** is False
g) **True**, False is False
h) **True, True** is **True**

Now, let's use 0.01 as a synonym of FALSE, and 0.99 as a synonym of TRUE.

We have got four patterns of two elements each (in 0.01-0.99 format):

Pattern **1**: {*0.01; 0.01*}
Expected value for training: <u>0.01</u>

Pattern **2**: {*0.01; 0.99*}
Expected value for training: <u>0.01</u>

Pattern **3**: {*0.99; 0.01*}
Expected value for training: <u>0.01</u>

Pattern **4**: {*0.99; 0.99*}
Expected value for training: <u>0.99</u>

So, each element can be identified if we know the layer, the row, and the column.

Examples:

- The first element of pattern 1 is element(1,1,1)
- The Expected value of this element is element(10,1,1)

View of the Input Patterns for this Example

Layer	Row	Column	Value	Comment
1	1	1	0.01	Pattern 1: 0.01-0.01
1	2	1	0.01	
1	1	2	0.01	Pattern 2: 0.01-0.99
1	2	2	0.99	
1	1	3	0.99	Pattern 3: 0.99-0.01
1	2	3	0.01	
1	1	4	0.99	Pattern 4: 0.99-0.99
1	2	4	0.99	
10	1	1	<u>0.01</u>	Target 1: "False"
10	1	2	<u>0.01</u>	Target 2: "False"
10	1	3	<u>0.01</u>	Target 3: "False"
10	1	4	<u>0.99</u>	Target 4: "True"

We can use any procedure we know to input the data into the table. We can directly use the Access program to do it and copy and paste the data into the table, or we can program a common graphic interface (a specific program) to do it. It is up to us. The important thing here is that we need to store the numbers before we operate the net.

PART III

Design of a Web-based
Neural Network

CHAPTER 4

What is a Web-based Neural Network?

It is a special type of Neural Network, specially made to be run on the Internet. Thus, it can be used as part of a web page, or included in a web site. This is perhaps the core section of this book.

Why we have to use them?

First of all: Why the Internet? Why do we have to place our net there?

The answer is simple: You do not have to do it, but you can use it to improve your work. The Internet offers us several advantages.

The net provides automatic access to our N-Net to users from all parts of the world. If we want to make something that could be used by a lot of people around the world, we have two options:

a) Give each of them a copy of the N-Net software, and instructions to install it locally. This is the typical option. However, this option requires a logistic infrastructure to work properly, such as a vast net of resellers, distributors, local VARs (value-added resellers), etc.

  •   The users need to have enough knowledge to install it or call some-one to install the net in their machines.

  •   They have to make it work with their local machines.

  •   Any new version or modification of the net has to be distributed. So, if any update is made to the software, the users will have to buy it and pay for it again.

b)   Publish your net on the web. In this case:

c)

- You only have to take care of your published net.
- You do not need a vast net of resellers.
- You do not need to install it.
- You can update the software as often as you want.
- You have instant access to the latest version.
- You do not have to buy any specific hardware. You can use the hardware that has been installed.

In other words: It is cheaper, more efficient, and easier to solve any problem if we use a Web-based Neural Network instead of a traditional one. The idea of this section is to give help and tricks to those readers who might want to make their own nets.

I have read many books about N-Nets, and one of the commonest failures is that the language used is extremely cryptic and confusing and the authors tell what they've done, not *how* they did it.

When I started to program N-Nets, I experienced a lot of failures and mistakes. In this section I'd like to talk about them and tell readers the tricks I discovered during that process. I expect this could be able to save you from hours (or days) of worthless work.

What do we do? Where do we start?

When I began to write the pages that you are reading, I did not really intend to write a book about Neural Networks for the Internet. I just was aiming to write a book about N-Nets. That is all. I do not know if there is a standard procedure to write technical books, but in my case (before writing a book), I first programmed every software or example that will be described. My books are essentially factual. I write about what I have experienced by myself. Thus, I looked for a flexible environment in which to develop the net. I wanted to include a net in this book, for those readers who might wish to program one by themselves. I also wanted to show them something working, something about which they could say, "That's right, *this is the example shown in the book.*" There was even more restrictions: My aim was to make something that could be easy to install. I did not want users to waste their time installing the net, and I also wish that they have access to the latest version of the net (in case I decide to update it).

As a matter of fact, I consider Internet to be the clearest tool to perform said work with all the characteristics I have already mentioned.

At this point, I started to program the environment, the nets, and the examples for the Internet, but the purpose of the book itself was still the same (just a book about Neural Networks).

While I was programming the code, I noticed that there were several facts and tricks that had to be developed to make the net work in this particular environment, so I discovered that preparing the net for the Internet has some specifications that are unique. Finally I realized that it might be a good idea to write not only about N-Nets themselves, but also about how to make them for the Web.

In this chapter we will talk about these unique specifications I have mentioned. My intention is to let readers know my experience, as well as to let them save time on their own projects.

Designing a Web-based Neural Network. First approach to the problem.

Once you have decided to make a Neural Network for the Internet, the first question you have to ask yourself is: *"How do I do it?"* We will talk about this now.

Parts I and II of this book cover the basic concepts related to the theory of Neural Networks. So we should now know what we want to build.

Point 1: Language of the Net

One of the main concepts I would like to share is that as far as I am concerned, a neural network can be programmed in any modern computer language.

In ancient times, Artificial Intelligence languages like Lisp or Prolog were used in an exclusive way. It was supposed that if you were programming something related to AI, then you should write its code either in Lisp or in Prolog. The use of Lisp was preferred in America, and Prolog in Europe.

I used both of them many years ago when I learnt about AI, and I have discovered that their functions could easily be emulated in any computer language if you know how to do it. The inference motor of them does not guarantee you to have a better performance than the one you would get with a modern Object-oriented language. As a matter of fact, I have never wanted to be a prisoner of any computer environment, so I prefer to use the tools I like best. Nowadays we can feel free to use the technology we like. I personally prefer the Java-Script/Java environment or the VB-Script/ASP one because they were designed for the Internet and they give instant access to the web.

Point 2: Election of the Environment

When preparing a program for the Internet, we have two general environments to work with:

a) **A proprietary environment**: The Microsoft® environment is the most popular one. In this case you have to use Microsoft® software tools to program your application. You will need an HTML and a source code editor, such as FrontPage®, a Personal Web Server software to test your prototypes, such as Microsoft® IIS5 or a higher one (since the launch of Windows2000®, it comes with the installation CD-ROM; previous versions can be downloaded from the Microsoft® web site), and enough knowledge of a Server language such as ASP.

b) **An open environment**: It is based on the Unix-Linux open-source policy. Here you use free software languages and tools to build your net, such as Apache, PHP, etc.

The examples used in this book were made using the first environment. So, all the explanations will refer to this methodology, but this is not the only alternative.

Point 3: Hosting

The second thing you have to think about is where to host your net. You should have a paid or free hosting site to upload the net to.

Your first step is to create a site for your network(s). I have placed mine at:

http://www5.domaindlx.com/mgbosq/index.html

Point 4: Choosing the Architecture

As was said before, the most popular N-Net architecture is the Back-Propagation Network. However, it requires much time to be trained. When you design a Web-based Neural Network, you have to take care about a particular variable: TIME. This is an important subject to talk about. When you design traditional Neural Networks, you do not pay attention to it. In a web site, if the user has to wait too much for his response, he will get impatient.

The art of designing Web-based Neural Networks is related to the management of time.

In other words, you have to design the nets in such a way that they could show their results in an acceptable time. As an example, I have placed on the web site of this book two examples of the same Neural Network, a faster one and a slower one. You can download the source code from the page to see the differences. Both nets are the same, but one code is executed faster than the other one—in a visible way. Bear in mind that some aesthetic routines may be terrible time-consumers. So, when you design a Web-based Neural Network, always be aware of the time it takes to work.

By the way, you should know how to program in ASP and HTML before attempting to make your own Web-based net. There are lots of books that teach you how to do it if you are not a programmer. As I have written my own one entitled "Programming a Real Internet Site with HTML and ASP," it is obvious that I will recommend mine, but any good manual will be effective as well.

Point 5: Esthetic versus Speed

Sometimes you will have to sacrifice the way the page looks like to make it faster. In standard HTML pages, the designers always try to make them look attractive. The content is important, but the presentation and graphic design of the page are important too.

Nevertheless, this rule is not valid for a Web-based N-Net. It is better to design a standard and basic look for the page, because it will download faster, and time is money in the world wide web.

Point 6: Beware of Time-Consuming Java Scripts

As I said before in this chapter, I always try to program every example before I publish a book. I learn a lot from my failures. In my first attempt to make a web net, I wanted to design a user-friendly interface. I thought it could be great to have the net calculating the values online, and showing them to the users. In order to do that I created several text boxes in HTML, and I stored the main variables in them. The main page of the site started to look like this:

Time Out	Loops	Error	Pattern Size	Loaded Patterns
270	1000	0.025	15	4
Values				
{0.72754}	{0.75 }	{0.0044}	{0.022439}	{0.0026}
{0.124241}	{0.0456}	{0.424541}	{0.727841}	{0.234541}
{0.034546}	{0.064748}	{0.094949}	{0.954961}	{0.0345941}

The text boxes were called "train1," "train2," etc., and were part of a form called "trainnet1."

My idea was to let the values change online as soon as they were calculated. This would give the users the feeling of a difficult program to use. The effect worked all right. However, look at the code it generated in the HTML page:

Using Scripts to show the values online

```
<script>javascript:trainnet1.train1.value=-1</script>
<script>javascript:trainnet1.train2.value=0</script>
<script>javascript:trainnet1.train1.value=-1</script>
<script>javascript:trainnet1.train2.value=-2</script>
<script>javascript:trainnet1.train1.value=-1</script>
<script>javascript:trainnet1.train2.value=-2</script>
<script>javascript:trainnet1.train1.value=1</script>
<script>javascript:trainnet1.train2.value=2</script>
<script>javascript:trainnet1.train3.value=6</script>
<script>javascript:trainnet1.train4.value=1</script>
<script>javascript:trainnet1.train1.value=-1</script>
<script>javascript:trainnet1.train2.value=-2</script>
<script>javascript:trainnet1.train1.value=-1</script>
<script>javascript:trainnet1.train2.value=0</script>
<script>javascript:trainnet1.train1.value=-1</script>
<script>javascript:trainnet1.train2.value=0</script>
<script>javascript:trainnet1.train1.value=1</script>
<script>javascript:trainnet1.train2.value=0</script>
<script>javascript:trainnet1.train3.value=2</script>
<script>javascript:trainnet1.train4.value=1</script>
<script>javascript:trainnet1.train1.value=-1</script>
<script>javascript:trainnet1.train2.value=2</script>
<script>javascript:trainnet1.train1.value=1</script>
<script>javascript:trainnet1.train2.value=-2</script>
<script>javascript:trainnet1.train3.value=-6</script>
<script>javascript:trainnet1.train4.value=-1</script>
<script>javascript:trainnet1.train1.value=1</script>
```

The source code was increased exponentially!! Of course this makes the page execution exponentially slower.

So, one of the most important things you have to know is this: As we have said, there is a conflict between the look of the page and the time it consumes. The last one is an explicit example of this fact. Be extremely careful about the scripts you use in the page. Do not hesitate to sacrifice beauty if doing so makes the execution faster.

Point 7: Creating the Site: Frames

The net will be placed as functions or procedures in an ASP/HTML structure. This means that first of all, you will have to build the main page of your site, and the menus. The net itself will work in the mainframe of the site. I have made my site using this structure: A vertical menu lets the user choose the architecture of the net. When you select it, you will be executing the code included in the mainframe.

So, the page looks like this...

	Menu1	Menu2	Menu3	Menu4
Select architecture				
Net1	Mainframe			
Net2				
Net3				

If you want to design a site with only one kind of network included, you don't need this previous screen. The structure of your site might look like this:

		Menu1	Menu2	Menu3	Menu4
Home					
Load Sample	Show Patterns	Mainframe			
Max Error:					
Execute	Train				

The vertical menu lets you load sample patterns, show them or not, and switch between execution and training mode.

Steps to Design a Web-based Neural Network

In Chapter II we saw the different architectures and main concepts related to N-Nets. Here we will confirm which ones of them are needed to make the Web-based version of it.

The design of a Web-based Artificial Neural Network consists of the creation of an Internet site that could be able to:

I.   Start the Program

II. Dimension Arrays (depending on the network architecture)

III. Name the first array "Input Layer"

IV. Name the last array "Output Layer"

V.   Name the intermediate arrays "Hidden Layers"

VI. Read input patterns from a database or a graphic file and store them in the input-layer array

VII. If a database exists with input-layer weights, then store them in the input-layer weights array

VIII. If a database exists with output patterns then store them in the output layer array

IX. Propagate: For each hidden layer: Get values from the previous layer

X.   Calculate values emerging from the activation function

XI. Multiply these values by the weights of the layer

XII. Send the results to the next layer

XIII. Send results of the last hidden layer to the output layer

XIV. Read output layer values

XV. Seek in the output description database the meaning in words of the output values

XVI. Send report to the network operator using the meaning of the output values

XVII. Execute the default program for the output value

XVIII. End network

The actions that can perform a software program based on the network's output can be:

•   Informative: The program informs that an answer for the input pattern has been found. Example: In a network designed to classify different sizes of bottles, the net uses as input the digital image taken from a video camera.

The camera focuses on a production line in which several different-sized bottles are circulating. The net has to recognize any size different from the standard ones and report this fact to the operator. The network input is then the digital image taken from the camera, and the output is the identification of the size of the bottle. An informative action could be the execution of a warning message onscreen each time that a bizarre bottle is found.

- Operative: In this case, after the warning message, the program executes some procedure. Going on with the example of the bottle classification, we could have an operative action if the program is attached to a robotic arm control, and it orders the arm to extract the bizarre bottle from the production line. As an alternative procedure, the computer could open a trapdoor in the production line and let the bottle fall down into a wastebasket.

- Predictive: In this case the program uses the network output to forecast the behavior of a variable. Example: A network with weather data as an input pattern could be used to make predictions about the future weather and then spread this information to the proper government agencies.

CHAPTER 5

Building the Network: Databases, Tables, Environmental Variables, and Main Functions

Databases: Defining where to store data

First of all, we will need a database to store the digital patterns. The ASP environment accepts an SQL Server or Access databases.

Many authors say that an SQL-Server or MySQL databases are the best ones, but I personally did not have any trouble with Access databases. (I have used large files in my life.) I do not know if the ones who claim for SQL really mean that or if they are supporting the marketing effort of SQL's vendors. It is not the objective of this book to discuss which one is better. You should choose the one you like best.

There must be some kind of a capture device like a scanner or a video camera. This device captures the pattern, digitalizes it, and stores the binary string in a file.

There are two ways to load the patterns:

a) The operator manually fills the database with the patterns. (In other words, he copies and pastes the strings into the database.) This is the easiest way for someone who is practicing.

b) There is a software program that does it automatically.

As this is just a secondary operation, we will assume that this operation has already been done.

Data Structure

Our data will be located as tables in our database, each of which contains fields where the data will be placed.

Trick: It is useful to use permanent data tables and temporal data tables.

Permanent Storage Tables

a) BPN-Original. To store all input patterns. It contains the fields: *Layer-number, row, column, value, pattern-code-name*

We can write the pattern number in the columns (for example) and the pattern items in the rows.

Example: Suppose we have three strings:

1) "000111000" corresponding to "Shape1"
2) "000000111" corresponding to "Shape2"
3) "111000000" corresponding to "Shape3"

Each string has 9 elements, so we have three patterns of three items. If we design "1" to the input layer, our first record of the table would be the following:

> *Layer-number:* 1
>
> *Row:* 1 (First element)
>
> *Column:* 1 (First string)
>
> *Value:* **0** (the first element of the first string has value 0)
>
> *Pattern-name:* Shape1 (The name of the first string)
>
> In other words, we will have a table with 27 records (3 shapes x 9 elements).

So, at this point we have a database with the BPN-original table filled with the patterns we want the net to recognize. A real-life professional network may have patterns of 100000-1000000 (or more) elements. If we consider that each pixel of a graphic file is an element, a file of 200K contains more than 200000 pixels. This excessive number of items makes the net run extremely slow if you are not using a mainframe.

However, the network design and architecture are the same, independent of the number of items of the patterns. That is the reason why in this book we will focus on the network architecture and we will use small sample patterns to work with. They make the network run faster and do not interfere with the way it is made.

b) BPN-Weights-Original. To store all weights. It contains the same structure as BPN-Original. At the beginning, the net is not trained, so the table is filled with random values. Once the net is trained, the values make the input pattern recognizable. These values are stored here. If these values were not stored, we would have to train it each time the net has to be run. (The training is a very time-consuming process.) It is a good idea to save the weighs values in a permanent table apart from the actual work table. Sometimes, when we train the network a new input pattern degrades the performance of the weights and it is not unusual for us to try on again. In those moments we need an original (untouched) version of the weights. That is the reason why I have created two tables: this one and a second one called BPN-weights that is just used to work with the actual pattern.

Trick: Many N-nets just return an insipid value like "0.123456." This says nothing for the user. It is useful to have a "targets" table where the net should seek to have an answer like "The pattern corresponds to a B2 Stealth Bomber Airplane."

c) Targets-Original. To store all target values. It contains three fields: Target-number, Target-name, and Target-value.

Example: If we have three possible answers, our first record of the table would be the following:

> *Target-number:* 1
>
> *Target-name:* *"Centered pattern"* (name of the element)
>
> *Target-value:* 0,9

This means that if the network processes an input pattern and it calculates a value of 0.9 for it, the net has to answer that the pattern is a "Centered pattern," or whatever we place as a target-name. If the patterns correspond to military airplane shapes, a target name could be *"F14 Tomcat."*

Temporary Working Tables

(Temporary tables just to work in a single network search)

Table 1: **BPN.** To store the input pattern we are working with. It has the same structure as BPN-Original.

Table 2: **BPN-weights.** To store the weights we are working with. It has the same structure as BPN-Weights-Original.

Table 3: **Targets.** To store target values we are working with. It has the same structure as Targets-Original.

Environmental Variables

Like any system, the network will need some variables to work properly. We will have eight variables—Text1 to Text8—to store temporary values.

Example:

Text1Text = ""   'reserved for later use
Text2Text = 9   '*maximum size of each pattern*
Text3Text = 8   '*total number of patterns stored in the database*
Text4Text = 3   'hidden *weight layer size*
Text5Text = 6   'current pattern number
Text6Text = 0.025   'minimum acceptable error
Text7Text = 1000   'number of iterations before finishing training
Text8Text = 0.5   'learning speed

Maximum Size of Patterns

When the net loads the inputs, it counts the size of each one and stores in this variable the maximum length. (The number of elements that each pattern has.) It is important that all the strings may have the same number of elements. If some have few items, the difference must be filled with "0" values.

The maximum pattern size allowed depends on the network and the hardware environment. If the N-net operator discovers that the performance slows dramatically beyond some number of items per string, then this value must be set up as a limit and the net architecture has to be changed, if necessary.

Total Number of Patterns

How many patterns does a N-Net recognize? As a matter of fact, the number varies depending on the architecture of the network. In a N-Net that recognizes military airplane shapes, the number of patterns means the quantity of planes that the net can detect. The N-Net may also extract this value from the database counting the records stored. In general, N-Nets work properly with a small number of strings and their performance starts to decay beyond some point. We can add more length to the hidden layers to increase the number of shapes, but this has an exponential effect on the net speed.

It is worthless to have a net that distinguishes all the shapes required. This could be so slow that people might not want to use it. When these cases happen, the network operator might think seriously of using another architecture like a PHN, which has parallel hidden layers, each one with its own weights. In this case the number of shapes may be increased proportionally to the number of hidden layers.

Hidden Weight Layer Size

The hidden layer can have a user-defined length. The effect that a longer weight layer may cause in terms of effectiveness must be seen in each case. Not always does a bigger hidden layer mean a better recognition system, but in general a heavier hidden layer means a poor and slow N-Net.

Current Pattern Number

When we train the network, we must use all of the database patterns. This variable shows the actual pattern number we are using. If we are just executing the net, it shows the number of the pattern recognized.

Minimum Acceptable Error

This is useful only in the training process. A 0.0025 value means an acceptable error of 0,25 percent. The network operator must identify the tolerance of the N-Net recognition in terms of the percentage of error it may admit.

This concept must be understood properly: If we increase the error value, the net will be able to recognize "similar" shapes to the one stored in the database. If we input an airplane image whose shape is similar to the one stored, the net will recognize it anyway. However, the net will also be able to identify false shapes as valid ones. A large bird or a delta-wing could be recognized as an airplane, for example.

Trick: Make several proofs with different error values to calibrate the network in such a way that it may be able to recognize the correct patterns.

Number of iterations before we End Training

Trick: Use an iteration counter in your net to prevent the training processes from becoming too slow.

This is a variable that the experience has taught me to use. When we use the above method of the minimum error to train the N-Net, we are saying to it:

"Run the training algorithm until the error is equal to or less than the minimum error."

This is the standard method to train the net. However, I have seen that some nets may delay for hours or days doing it. If the programmer detects that the net is spending too much time on being trained, we can program a safety clause that says:

"Stop training if more than 1000 iterations have been made and the error is still bigger than the minimum expected one."

In these cases, I have seen that it is useful to reconsider the environment variables or some of the network architecture to set it up in a more synchronic way with the reality. Perhaps we are using patterns that are too similar and we must think about diversity. Perhaps the patterns are too big and the net uses too much time calculating. We might see the opportunity to use shorter strings and then see the results.

In DNA pattern recognition, only less than 1 percent of the pattern is used, because the DNA molecule is so big that it is nearly impossible to work with all of it.

Learning Speed

This is a variable that takes control of the network learning. The net can be configured to learn the new patterns fast, but this action has a risk. If the process is too fast, the net will forget the old strings of its memory.

Trick: It is advisable to set up an intermediate learning speed for the net.

Main Functions

Remember: We have two processes that can be done by the same program or by different programs.

    a)   Training of the N-Net
    b)   Running (search for data) of the net

We must train the net to get the right weights for the patterns each time we add a new shape to the net database, but once we have made it, we just use it. That means we have to make the net run to let it recognize the input pattern.

If we have two separate modules—one for training and one for running—then the main function of a BPN for running must:

    a)   Set up the tables, load the input data and the weighs into the net, and give initial values to the environment variables
    b)   Make a forward propagation of the input pattern
    c)   Get the output value for that input
    d)   Send a message to the operator displaying that value

A main function in ASP would look like this:

```
Function bpn(bpnpattern)

'BPN for Running only. No training

st = setup-tables()
if st = true then
forwardpropagate(bpnpattern)
bpn = getoutput()
MsgBox "Output of pattern " & Str(bpnpattern) & " is: " & Str(bpn)

End if

End Function
```

If we prefer to make the net train the weights, then the main function would be the following:

```
Function bpn2(bpnpattern, limit)

'BPN execution complete. Includes training

Do While Net-Error > limit
Setup-tables()
forwardpropagate(bpnpattern) 'requires pattern number

calc-output-error (Text4.Text)
adjust-weights()
Loop
Bpn2 = "Network Trained for pattern: & str(bpnpattern)
End function
```

These are just examples of a main function. The complete source code can be found at the author's web site:

"http://www5.domaindlx.com/mgbosq/index.html" section downloads. If you can't find the site, email the author at mgbosq@sinectis.com.ar and ask him if he has changed its URL.

CHAPTER 6

Using the Net
Sample Exercises

These sample exercises are a part of a Web-based Neural Network which is published at:

http://www5.domaindlx.com/mgbosq/indexnnets.html.[1]

As readers of this book, you are allowed to use it as a sample test site. There you will find an environment to see these samples working, and to download the source code if you like. The net requires a password to enter: use "1949" as a valid one.

Here we will explain a bit about how to use it.

For each example you have got three steps to do:

a) Load one of the sample patterns. (Step 1)

b) Train the net with these patterns loaded. (Step 2)

c) Once the net is trained, choose a specific pattern (Step 3) and execute the net.

---

[1] If you can't find the site, email the author at mgbosq@sinectis.com.ar and ask him if he has changed its URL.

d) Compare the answer of it with the expected value to see if the training worked.

e) Once the net is trained, you only have to load a pattern into Data1 table and execute the net to verify whether the pattern is recognized or not. Data 1 is a table of an Access database. You can use Access to modify/add the values of it.

Exercises:

The web site contains several architectures to work with. This part of the book explains them deeply. If the Sample Exercise does not mention the architecture used to run it, take for granted that it was a BPN.

Sample Exercise #1: Telling the Net to Recognize Shapes

Here we have got four patterns, the patterns of geometrical shapes. We will work with a circle, a square, sole lines, and an X. In order to work with shapes, it is easy if we create tables, with rows and columns, and we assign values to each cell. We can use a blank or null value when there are blank spaces in the shape, and we can use some solid character to fill the other cells.

In these examples, I have made shapes using asterisks. Big networks use the same principle, but they use the pixels of an image instead of asterisks. The only difference is that they need to have networks with bigger arrays, and bigger computers to calculate the values. However, the net itself is the same. Once you have got the pattern, you have to convert it into a binary code made with 0s and 1s. This causes a bit of trouble because when we multiply any number by 0m, the result is 0, so the network gets confused, and we need more nodes to run it properly. We can just solve it by using 0.01 and 0.99 instead of 0 and 1.

In our example, we have got the following:

Pattern				Name	Conversion to 0.01-0.99			
	*	*			0.01	0.99	0.99	0.01
*			*		0.99	0.01	0.01	0.99
*			*	Circle	0.99	0.01	0.01	0.99
*			*		0.99	0.01	0.01	0.99
	*	*			0.01	0.99	0.99	0.01
*	*	*	*		0.99	0.99	0.99	0.99
*			*		0.99	0.01	0.01	0.99
*			*	Square	0.99	0.01	0.01	0.99
*			*		0.99	0.01	0.01	0.99
*	*	*	*		0.99	0.99	0.99	0.99
*	*	*	*		0.99	0.99	0.99	0.99
					0.01	0.01	0.01	0.01
*	*	*	*	Lines	0.99	0.99	0.99	0.99
					0.01	0.01	0.01	0.01
*	*	*	*		0.99	0.99	0.99	0.99
					0.01	0.01	0.01	0.01
*			*		0.99	0.01	0.01	0.99
	*	*		X	0.01	0.99	0.99	0.01
	*	*			0.01	0.99	0.99	0.01
*			*		0.99	0.01	0.01	0.99

If we call the circle "Pattern 1," the square "Pattern 2," etc., we will have the following:

Pattern	Node	Value	Pattern	Node	Value
1	1	0.01	3	1	0.99
1	1	0.99	3	1	0.5
1	2	0.99	3	2	0.99
1	3	0.99	3	3	0.99
1	4	0.01	3	4	0.99
1	5	0.99	3	5	0.01
1	6	0.01	3	6	0.01
1	7	0.01	3	7	0.01
1	8	0.99	3	8	0.01
1	9	0.99	3	9	0.01
1	10	0.01	3	10	0.01
1	11	0.01	3	11	0.01
1	12	0.99	3	12	0.01
1	13	0.01	3	13	0.99
1	14	0.99	3	14	0.99
1	15	0.99	3	15	0.99
1	16	0.01	3	16	0.99
2	1	0.99	4	1	0.01
2	1	0.3	4	1	0.99
2	2	0.99	4	2	0.01
2	3	0.99	4	3	0.01
2	4	0.99	4	4	0.01
2	5	0.99	4	5	0.99
2	6	0.01	4	6	0.01
2	7	0.01	4	7	0.01
2	8	0.99	4	8	0.99
2	9	0.99	4	9	0.01
2	10	0.01	4	10	0.99
2	11	0.01	4	11	0.99
2	12	0.99	4	12	0.01
2	13	0.99	4	13	0.99
2	14	0.99	4	14	0.01
2	15	0.99	4	15	0.01
2	16	0.99	4	16	0.99

All of these are the values that must be inserted in the input layer (layer number 1). We have to then create the main table to input the patterns and the expected values for training to the net. We can use an Access or SQL Server Database. We will call this table BPN. The structure of it is then the following:

BPN (Layer, Row, Column, Value, Comment) in the English version, or
BPN (Capa, Fila, Columna, Valor, Nombre) in the Spanish version

---

Table BPN—Field Structure

Layer: We will store a "1" in the field "layer" to let the net know that these values are from layer 1, or input layer

Row: The nodes will be stored here

Column: It contains the pattern numbers

Value: The digital value of the node

Comment: Any comment about the node

Example: The first element of the first pattern of the input layer will have the following values:

Element 1:

Layer: 1
Row: 1
Column: 1
Value: 0.01
Comment: Pattern "Circle"

We can now add the expected output layers (layer number 10), so we have got our input table:

Layer	Row	Column	Value	Comment
10	1	1	0	Layer
10	2	1	0,3	10
10	3	1	0,5	Means
10	4	1	0,8	Output Expected Values
				For patterns 1,2,3 & 4

You can see an example of the complete table at Appendix A, at the end of the book.

-------------0-------------

What Happens when we Execute the Net?

After that, I have measured the results. The output values are the ones that the net answered when it was executed. The difference is calculated as the difference between the expected values and the output ones. If the net answered CIRCLE when CIRCLE was expected, the difference is zero. If "SQUARE" was expected and the net answered "CIRCLE," the difference is 1.

Finally, the differences are summed up. The net difference is the size of error that the net returned.

	Expected	Tolerance: Max Error=0.025	
Pattern	Target	Output value	Difference
1	Circle	Circle	0
2	Square	Square	0
3	Lines	Lines	0
4	X	X	0
Net difference:			0

As we see, the efficiency of the network to recognize basic shapes is excellent. All the patterns were recognized.

Looking at this example, we can deduce the following:

We have proved that we can use a Neural Network as a way to recognize basic shapes.

Sample Exercise #2: Teaching Logic to the Net

When we use the AND, OR, NOT, XOR operators in a formula, or when we are making a program, we say we are using logic operators. The question is the following: Can we teach the net to act like a logic operator? Let us see…

We are going to teach the AND operator to the net. The AND operator works with two logic premises, generally called A and B. With them we make the AND table as follows:

If **A** is true and **B** is true, we can say that **A AND B** are true. Otherwise, **A AND B** are false.

In other words:

AND Operator

A	B	A and B
True	True	True
True	False	False
False	True	False
False	False	False

Here we will represent the A and B premises as nodes of a pattern. Since we cannot use letters in the net, we will replace A and B with "0.1" and "0.9," so "0.1" will be "A" and "0.9" will be "B." The target will be the expected result of the AND operator. In other words, we will use four patterns. We will use 0.1 as True, and = 0.9 as False. Thus, when the net gives us an output of 0.1, we will say it is true. When the net gives us an output of 0.9, we will say it is false.

The inputs will be the following:

Pattern	Premises	Value
1	1	0,1
1	2	0,1
2	1	0,1
2	2	0,9
3	1	0,9
3	2	0,1
4	1	0,9
4	2	0,9

The target (expected outputs) will then be the following:

Target	Value
1	0,1
2	0,1
3	0,1
4	0,9

What do these tables mean? Very simple: We have got four patterns called 1, 2, 3, and 4. Each pattern has two nodes that are represented by a row, so each pattern has two rows. The nodes represent the premises A or B, and each node has a value of 0,1 or 0,9. So:

Pattern	Premises	Value
1	1	0,1
1	2	0,1

This means that the pattern 1 has two nodes (premises).

The premise A (or 1) is False (0,1).
The premise B (or 2) is False (0,1).

If we see the target of the pattern 1, we will find the following:

Pattern	Value
1	0,1

In other words, we are saying that if A is false and B is false, then A AND B are false too.

Now, let us say "Column" for the pattern column, and "Row" for the premise column. This is just to make our table compatible with the data definitions of the executable program. So, we have got the following:

Row	Column	Value
1	1	0,1
2	1	0,1
1	2	0,1
2	2	0,9
1	3	0,9
2	3	0,1
1	4	0,9
2	4	0,9

For outputs, we have the following:

1	1	0,1
1	2	0,1
1	3	0,1
1	4	0,9

In this table, we have placed the inputs and the expected outputs of the patterns to do the training. We should also have another field to let the program know which data belongs to the input layer and which belongs to the expected targets. We will here adopt the following rule: We will add a new field called "layer." It will have the value "1" for the input layer and "10" for the expected targets. We have even created a field to store comments or labels to the patterns. Our table will look like this one:

Layer	Row	Column	Value	Comment
1	1	1	0,1	Pattern 1: False-False
1	2	1	0,1	
1	1	2	0,1	Pattern 2: False-True
1	2	2	0,9	
1	1	3	0,9	Pattern 3: True-False
1	2	3	0,1	
1	1	4	0,9	Pattern 4: True-True
1	2	4	0,9	
10	1	1	0,1	Target 1: False
10	1	2	0,1	Target 2: False
10	1	3	0,1	Target 3: False
10	1	4	0,9	Target 4: True

What happens when we execute it? Well, the following table shows us the results:

The first column shows us the patterns of the AND Sample Example. The second one is the value we are expecting the net to answer. In other words, pattern 1 is False-False, so the net should return the "False" value.

After that, I have measured the results. The output values are the ones that the net answered when it was executed. The difference is calculated as the difference that the net answered. That means: If the net answered FALSE when FALSE was expected, the difference is zero. If "FALSE" was expected and the net answered TRUE, the difference is 1.

Finally, the differences are summed up. The net difference is the magnitude of error that the net returned.

Pattern	Expected Target	Tolerance: Max Error = 0.025	
		Output value	Difference
1	FALSE	False	0
2	FALSE	False	0
3	FALSE	False	0
4	TRUE	True	0
Net difference:			0

As we see, the efficiency of the network for this example is 100 percent consistent. All the patterns were recognized.

Looking at this example, we can deduce the following:

> We can use a Neural Network as a way to simulate logic operators.

Sample Exercise #3: Teaching the Net How to Recognize Numbers

In this sample we are going to teach a BPN the numbers from 1 to 9; 1, 2, 3, through 9. In other words, there will be nine patterns. The net has to recognize which number is which. Notice that we are just entering the shape of the numbers through the keyboard. We will use the 0.01-0.99 format:

Here are the patterns and their digital translation:

PATTERN 1

```
    *          0.01 0.01 0.99 0.01
  * *          0.01 0.99 0.99 0.01
    *          0.01 0.01 0.99 0.01
    *          0.01 0.01 0.99 0.01
```

PATTERN 2

```
  * * *        0.01 0.99 0.99 0.99
  *   *        0.01 0.99 0.01 0.99
    *          0.01 0.01 0.99 0.01
  * * *        0.01 0.99 0.99 0.99
```

PATTERN 3

```
  * * *        0.01 0.99 0.99 0.99
    * *        0.01 0.01 0.99 0.99
      *        0.01 0.01 0.01 0.99
  * * *        0.01 0.99 0.99 0.99
```

PATTERN 4

```
*       *          0.99  0.01  0.01  0.99
*       *          0.99  0.01  0.01  0.99
* * * *            0.99  0.99  0.99  0.99
        *          0.01  0.01  0.01  0.99
```

PATTERN 5

```
* * *              0.01  0.99  0.99  0.99
*                  0.01  0.99  0.01  0.01
    * *            0.01  0.01  0.99  0.99
* * *              0.01  0.99  0.99  0.99
```

PATTERN 6

```
* *                0.01  0.99  0.99  0.01
*                  0.99  0.01  0.01  0.01
* * * *            0.99  0.99  0.99  0.99
* * * *            0.99  0.99  0.99  0.99
```

PATTERN 7

```
* * * *            0.99  0.99  0.99  0.99
    *              0.01  0.01  0.99  0.01
  *                0.01  0.99  0.01  0.01
*                  0.99  0.01  0.01  0.01
```

PATTERN 8

```
* * * *            0.99  0.99  0.99  0.99
  * *              0.01  0.99  0.99  0.01
  * *              0.01  0.99  0.99  0.01
* * * *            0.99  0.99  0.99  0.99
```

PATTERN 9

```
* * *              0.01  0.99  0.99  0.99
* * *              0.01  0.99  0.99  0.99
    *              0.01  0.01  0.01  0.99
  * *              0.01  0.99  0.99  0.01
```

Results:

Again, I have measured the results. The output values are the ones that the net answered when it was executed. The difference is calculated as the difference between the output values and the expected ones. That means the following: If the net answered as it was expected to, the difference is zero. If it was expected to answer "1," and the net answered the next digit ("2"), the difference is 1. If it was expected to answer "2," and the net answers the previous value ("1"), then the difference is -1.

At the bottom of it, the differences are summed up. The net difference is the magnitude of error that the net returned.

Pattern	Expected Target	Tolerance: Max Error = 0.025		Tolerance: Max Error = 0.020		Tolerance: Max Error = 0.015	
		Output value	Dif	Output value	Dif	Output value	Dif
1	1	1	0	1	0	1	0
2	2	2	0	2	0	2	0
3	3	3	0	3	1	3	0
4	4	4	0	4	0	4	0
5	5	6	1	5	0	5	0
6	6	6	0	6	0	6	0
7	7	8	-1	8	0	7	0
8	8	8	0	8	9	8	0
9	9	8	1	9	1	9	0
Net difference:			1		1		0:

What happened here? The results were not 100 percent effective!!

One of the effects that you will notice in a network is that its performance suffers some degradation when you start to add more patterns to be recognized. As a matter of fact, it seems that BPNs are prepared just to recognize a few patterns each.

One of the solutions to this problem is to be stricter when we train the net. In order to see the this effect, the net was trained with a maximum error tolerance of 0.025 (2.5 percent), 0.020 (2 percent), and 0.015 (1.5 percent). We see here that the best net value was found under a 1.5 percent, so we can deduce that if we are stricter with the tolerance of the net, we will find a better performance.

Another solution is to make an attempt with other architecture, as a network with parallel hidden layers (PHL). Let us suppose we load the patterns 1 to 5 in the first parallel hidden layer, and the patterns 6 to 9 in the second one. In this case, the results would be the following:

Pattern	Expected Target	Tolerance: Max Error=0.025	
		Output value	Difference
1	1	1	0
2	2	2	0
3	3	3	0
4	4	4	0
5	5	5	0
6	6	6	0
7	7	7	0
8	8	8	0
9	9	9	0
Net difference:			0

Looking at this example, we can deduce the following:

Some architectures are more appropriate than others for a specific problem.

Sample Exercise #4: Teaching the Net to Read

ABC recognition. Here, the idea is to train the net to recognize the alphabet. We will first try it on a BPN, and then with a PHL.

You will be given 26 patterns, each one meaning a letter. The net has to return the letter that corresponds with that pattern. Once we have got the pattern, we will replace the blank spaces with "0" and the others with "1." However, when we multiply by zero, the result is zero, so "0" and "1" are not the proper values to work with. It is advisable to use 0.1 meaning zero, and 0.9 meaning 1, instead. So, the real input values will be strings containing values of 0.1 and 0.9.

Here it is the pattern for the letter "A" and the translation of it to the 0.1-0.9 syntax:

	*	*		0.1 0.9 0.9 0.1
*			*	0.9 0.1 0.1 0.9
*	*	*	*	0.9 0.9 0.9 0.9
*			*	0.9 0.1 0.1 0.9
*			*	0.9 0.1 0.1 0.9

The complete set of patterns can be found at Appendix B, at the end of the book.

What happens when we execute it with a BPN?

Results: The difference is calculated as the difference (in letters) that the net answered. That means the following: If the net answered as it was expected to, the difference is zero. If it was expected to answer "A," and the net answered the next letter ("B"), the difference is 1. This is the number of letters in the alphabet that we find between the expected value and the real output. If it was expected to answer "E", and the net answers the previous value ("D"), then the difference is -1.

Finally, the differences are summed up. The net difference is the magnitude of error that the net returned. In order to see the effect of the number of iterations, the net was trained at 1000, 2000, and 10000 iterations. We can see here that the best output value was found when we train the net using fewer than 1000 iterations. We can deduce that if we increase the training iterations, we will not find a better performance.

NET: BPN	Exp	Tolerance: Max Error= 0.025		Tolerance: Max Error= 0.020		Tolerance: Max Error= 0.015	
Pattern	Target	Output value	Dif	Output value	Dif	Output value	Dif
1	A	B	1	b	1	a	0
2	B	B	0	b	0	b	0
3	C	D	1	d	1	d	1
4	D	E	1	d	0	d	0
5	E	D	-1	e	0	d	-1
6	F	F	0	f	0	f	0
7	G	g	0	g	0	g	0
8	H	q	9	q	9	q	9
9	I	j	1	j	1	j	1
10	J	o	5	k	1	k	1
11	K	o	4	k	0	k	0
12	L	n	2	l	0	l	0
13	M	o	2	m	0	m	0
14	N	o	1	n	0	n	0
15	O	p	1	o	0	o	0
16	P	q	1	p	0	p	0
17	Q	q	0	q	0	p	-1
18	R	s	1	r	0	r	0
19	S	s	0	s	0	r	-1
20	T	o	-5	r	-2	u	1
21	U	u	0	u	0	u	0
22	V	t	-2	u	-1	u	-1
23	W	t	-3	q	-6	u	-2
24	x	q	-7	q	-7	q	-7
25	y	u	-4	u	-4	u	-4
26	Z	u	-5	u	-5	u	-5
Net difference:			3		-12		-9

As we may presume after the last example, the results were not 100 percent effective...

We have noted that in a BPN the performance suffers some degradation when you start to add more patterns to be recognized. As a matter of fact, it seems that biological neural nets are prepared to just recognize a few patterns each. What the brain does is multiply the number of nets it has got.

In other words, instead of one bigger network that recognizes all the patterns at the same time, we can have several small nets, each one able to recognize a few letters. If a net does not recognize the pattern, then it is delivered to the next ones until the pattern is recognized by any of them. Let us think in a net that just recognizes vowels. This would be a smaller net. If a pattern is a vowel, the net will recognize it. If it is not, then we use it as an input pattern for a second one, which just recognizes letters B to H (without the vowels). A third net just recognizes letters J to Z (without vowels). Think in a PHL with multiple hidden layers that could be able to do that…This could be a nice example for you to perform.

EPILOGUE

The study of neural networks offers a field of useful investigation to those people that are interested in creating computational models which could execute "intelligent" functions that were previously limited to humans. As new models and architectures are developed, Neural Networks are expected to be able to help people with their daily process of existence. The author hopes that the data and concepts supplied in this work will give the lay reader a brief understanding of the subject.

The language and terms used in this book have been fashioned to be accessible to ordinary people, although the complexity of the subject leads us to the use of many specific words related to the neural network world.

Source Code for a Sample Neural Network

As has been said, the readers of this book have access to a web site at:

http://www5.domaindlx.com/mgbosq/indexnnets.html[2]

On said site you can find a complete Web-based N-Net, and the source code to do it. Please use the password "1949" to enter the net.

---

[2] If you can't access this URL, email the author at mgbosq@sinectis.com.ar and ask him if the URL has changed.

CONCLUSIONS

Where are we now?

What have we learnt from all of this?

The study of the neural networks shows us a paradox:

First of all, we can say that many goals have been reached in this field. N-Nets are a reality today.

Many of them are already working around the world and they are being used for many things. Very well-known enterprises claim that they use systems based on neural networks to improve their operative performance.

However, the topic is still widely unknown. At the moment, all we can do with the neural networks is to make them recognize a few specific patterns.

If a net recognizes people's faces, for example, it is not able to recognize animals' shapes as well.

On the other hand we have the human brain, which is an all-purpose pattern recognition system. Any human being is able to recognize hundreds of shapes and patterns every day. We do it all the time—and fast!

At the moment I am writing this book, I have got on my desk a computer, a keyboard, a mouse, a plastic glass, a spoon, a sugar pot, etc. All of these things are shapes, patterns that I have recognized using my biological neural network. I did it in just a second, as everybody can. A two-year-old child can do it as well.

However, the strongest artificial neural network made up to now is far away from doing something similar.

Briefly speaking: The ultimate goal of neural networks remains to be reached.

N-Nets are a field for the future. We have got more research to do. The field of study is far from being complete.

As a matter of fact, it is open for every researcher who is interested in it. We are still raiders of the lost arc, searching for the sacred grail of technology. An artificial machine that is able to think, a Dr. Frankenstein's monster of real life, is a promise still to come.

Appendix A

Input Layer: Complete table to store the patterns

Layer	Row	Column	Value	Comment
1	1	1	0.01	
1	2	1	0.99	Pattern
1	3	1	0.99	1
1	4	1	0.99	Is
1	5	1	0.99	The
1	6	1	0.01	Circle
1	7	1	0.01	
1	8	1	0.99	
1	9	1	0.99	
1	10	1	0.01	
1	11	1	0.01	
1	12	1	0.99	
1	13	1	0.01	
1	14	1	0.99	
1	15	1	0.99	
1	16	1	0.01	
1	1	2	0.99	
1	2	2	0.99	
1	3	2	0.99	Pattern
1	4	2	0.99	2
1	5	2	0.99	Is
1	6	2	0.01	The
1	7	2	0.01	Square
1	8	2	0.99	
1	9	2	0.99	
1	10	2	0.01	
1	11	2	0.01	

Layer	Row	Column	Value	Comment
1	12	2	0.99	
1	13	2	0.99	
1	14	2	0.99	
1	15	2	0.99	
1	16	2	0.99	
1	1	3	0.99	Pattern
1	2	3	0.99	3
1	3	3	0.99	Are
1	4	3	0.99	Lines
1	5	3	0.01	
1	6	3	0.01	
1	7	3	0.01	
1	8	3	0.01	
1	9	3	0.01	
1	10	3	0.01	
1	11	3	0.01	
1	12	3	0.01	
1	13	3	0.99	
1	14	3	0.99	
1	15	3	0.99	
1	16	3	0.99	
1	1	4	0.01	
1	2	4	0.01	Pattern
1	3	4	0.01	4
1	4	4	0.01	Is
1	5	4	0.99	An X
1	6	4	0.01	
1	7	4	0.01	
1	8	4	0.99	
1	9	4	0.01	
1	10	4	0.99	
1	11	4	0.99	
1	12	4	0.01	
1	13	4	0.99	
1	14	4	0.01	
1	15	4	0.01	
1	16	4	0.99	

Layer	Row	Column	Value	Comment
10	1	1	0	Layer
10	2	1	0,3	10
10	3	1	0,5	Means
10	4	1	0,8	Output Expected Values
				For patterns 1,2,3 & 4

Appendix B

ABC Recognition: Complete set of patterns

```
  *  *        0.1 0.9 0.9 0.1
*        *    0.9 0.1 0.1 0.9
*  *  *  *    0.9 0.9 0.9 0.9
*        *    0.9 0.1 0.1 0.9
*        *    0.9 0.1 0.1 0.9

*  *  *       0.9 0.9 0.9 0.1
*        *    0.9 0.1 0.1 0.9
*  *  *  *    0.9 0.9 0.9 0.9
*        *    0.9 0.1 0.1 0.9
*  *  *  *    0.9 0.9 0.9 0.9

*  *  *  *    0.9 0.9 0.9 0.9
*            0.9 0.1 0.1 0.1
*            0.9 0.1 0.1 0.1
*            0.9 0.1 0.1 0.1
*  *  *  *    0.9 0.9 0.9 0.9

*  *  *       0.9 0.9 0.9 0.1
*        *    0.9 0.1 0.1 0.9
*        *    0.9 0.1 0.1 0.9
*        *    0.9 0.1 0.1 0.9
*  *  *       0.9 0.9 0.9 0.1
```

```
*   *   *   *        0.9 0.9 0.9 0.9
*                    0.9 0.1 0.1 0.1
*   *   *            0.9 0.9 0.9 0.1
*                    0.9 0.1 0.1 0.1
*   *   *   *        0.9 0.9 0.9 0.9

*   *   *   *        0.9 0.9 0.9 0.9
*                    0.9 0.1 0.1 0.1
*   *   *            0.9 0.9 0.9 0.1
*                    0.9 0.1 0.1 0.1
*                    0.9 0.1 0.1 0.1

    *   *   *        0.1 0.9 0.9 0.9
*                    0.9 0.1 0.1 0.1
*       *   *        0.9 0.1 0.9 0.9
*           *        0.9 0.1 0.1 0.9
*   *   *            0.9 0.9 0.9 0.1

*           *        0.9 0.1 0.1 0.9
*           *        0.9 0.1 0.1 0.9
*   *   *   *        0.9 0.9 0.9 0.9
*           *        0.9 0.1 0.1 0.9
*           *        0.9 0.1 0.1 0.9

    *                0.1 0.9 0.1 0.1
    *                0.1 0.9 0.1 0.1
    *                0.1 0.9 0.1 0.1
    *                0.1 0.9 0.1 0.1
    *                0.1 0.9 0.1 0.1

        *            0.1 0.1 0.1 0.9
        *            0.1 0.1 0.1 0.9
        *            0.1 0.1 0.1 0.9
        *            0.1 0.1 0.1 0.9
    *   *            0.1 0.9 0.9 0.1
```

	*		*	0.1	**0.9**	0.1	**0.9**
	*	*		0.1	**0.9**	**0.9**	0.1
	*			0.1	**0.9**	0.1	0.1
	*	*		0.1	**0.9**	**0.9**	0.1
	*		*	0.1	**0.9**	0.1	**0.9**
*				**0.9**	0.1	0.1	0.1
*				**0.9**	0.1	0.1	0.1
*				**0.9**	0.1	0.1	0.1
*				**0.9**	0.1	0.1	0.1
*	*	*		**0.9**	**0.9**	**0.9**	0.1
*			*	**0.9**	0.1	0.1	**0.9**
*	*	*	*	**0.9**	**0.9**	**0.9**	**0.9**
*			*	**0.9**	0.1	0.1	**0.9**
*			*	**0.9**	0.1	0.1	**0.9**
*			*	**0.9**	0.1	0.1	**0.9**
*			*	**0.9**	0.1	0.1	**0.9**
*	*		*	**0.9**	**0.9**	0.1	**0.9**
*		*	*	**0.9**	0.1	**0.9**	**0.9**
*			*	**0.9**	0.1	0.1	**0.9**
*			*	**0.9**	0.1	0.1	**0.9**
	*	*		0.1	**0.9**	**0.9**	0.1
*			*	**0.9**	0.1	0.1	**0.9**
*			*	**0.9**	0.1	0.1	**0.9**
*			*	**0.9**	0.1	0.1	**0.9**
	*	*		0.1	**0.9**	**0.9**	0.1
	*	*		0.1	**0.9**	**0.9**	0.1
*			*	**0.9**	0.1	0.1	**0.9**
*	*	*		**0.9**	**0.9**	**0.9**	0.1
*				**0.9**	0.1	0.1	0.1
*				**0.9**	0.1	0.1	0.1

```
*   *   *   *        0.9 0.9 0.9 0.9
*           *        0.9 0.1 0.1 0.9
*           *        0.9 0.1 0.1 0.9
*   *   *   *        0.9 0.9 0.9 0.9
            *        0.1 0.1 0.1 0.9


*   *   *   *        0.9 0.9 0.9 0.9
*           *        0.9 0.1 0.1 0.9
*   *   *   *        0.9 0.9 0.9 0.9
*       *            0.9 0.1 0.9 0.1
*           *        0.9 0.1 0.1 0.9


    *   *   *        0.1 0.9 0.9 0.9
    *                0.1 0.9 0.1 0.1
        *            0.1 0.1 0.9 0.1
            *        0.1 0.1 0.1 0.9
    *   *   *        0.1 0.9 0.9 0.9


    *   *   *        0.1 0.9 0.9 0.9
        *            0.1 0.1 0.9 0.1
        *            0.1 0.1 0.9 0.1
        *            0.1 0.1 0.9 0.1
        *            0.1 0.1 0.9 0.1


    *       *        0.1 0.9 0.1 0.9
    *       *        0.1 0.9 0.1 0.9
    *       *        0.1 0.9 0.1 0.9
    *       *        0.1 0.9 0.1 0.9
    *   *   *        0.1 0.9 0.9 0.9


*           *        0.9 0.1 0.1 0.9
*           *        0.9 0.1 0.1 0.9
*           *        0.9 0.1 0.1 0.9
*           *        0.9 0.1 0.1 0.9
    *   *            0.1 0.9 0.9 0.1
```

```
*           *       0.9 0.1 0.1 0.9
*           *       0.9 0.1 0.1 0.9
*           *       0.9 0.1 0.1 0.9
*   *   *   *       0.9 0.9 0.9 0.9
*           *       0.9 0.1 0.1 0.9

*           *       0.9 0.1 0.1 0.9
*           *       0.9 0.1 0.1 0.9
    *   *           0.1 0.9 0.9 0.1
*           *       0.9 0.1 0.1 0.9
*           *       0.9 0.1 0.1 0.9

*           *       0.9 0.1 0.1 0.9
*           *       0.9 0.1 0.1 0.9
*   *   *   *       0.9 0.9 0.9 0.9
    *   *           0.1 0.9 0.9 0.1
    *   *           0.1 0.9 0.9 0.1

*   *   *   *       0.9 0.9 0.9 0.9
        *           0.1 0.1 0.9 0.1
    *               0.1 0.9 0.1 0.1
*                   0.9 0.1 0.1 0.1
*   *   *   *       0.9 0.9 0.9 0.9
```

About the Author

Dr. Marcelo Bosque(L.A.) is a graduate of the University of Buenos Aires, where he is currently an associate professor. He has conducted extensive research in the field of Artificial Intelligence.

Some of his research includes:

- Understanding 99% of Artificial Neural Networks (2002)
- Optimization methods based on Genetic Algorithms (1996)
- Expert Systems for Visual Languages (1995)
- Expert Systems for Forecasting Financial Analysis (1993)
- Expert Systems (1992)

In addition, he has published a book about programming in ASP and HTML for the Web, which can be useful for those who wish to learn how to program a Neural Network but who may have difficulty with the code. The title is:

- Programming a Real Internet Site with HTML & ASP (2002)

BIBLIOGRAPHY

Author	Description
Ackley, D.H.	(1985) *AConnectionist algorithm for genetic search*, page 120-140
Anderson, James & Rosenfeld, Edward	(1987) *Neuro-computing*, Cambridge MA MIT Press
Anderson, James & Rosenfeld, Edward	(1990) *Neuro-computing 2*, Cambridge MA MIT Press
Asimov, Isaac	(1989) *Thoughts about Thought: Essay* (In Asimov on Science, A 30-year retrospective 1959, 1989)
Asimov, Isaac	(1989) *Essay: More Thoughts about Thought.* (In Asimov on Science, A 30-year retrospective 1959, 1989)
Asimov, Isaac	(1989) *Essay: The Egg and The Shell*, Essay about the nature of neural connections; (In Asimov on Science, A 30-year retrospective 1959, 1989)

Author	Description
Axelrod, R	(1987) *The evolution of strategies in the iterated prisoner's dilemma.* In *Genetic algorithms and simulated annealing,* page 30-40. London: Pitman
Bosque, Marcelo	(2002) *Understanding 99% of Artificial Neural Networks: Introduction & Tricks* (Writers Club Press)
Bosque, Marcelo	(2002) *Programming a REAL Internet site with ASP & HTML* (Writers Club Press)
Brock, William A. & Hsieh, David A	(1990) *A Test for Nonlinear Dynamics,* Cambridge MA MIT Press
Burton, Robert M.	(1991) *Event-Dependent Control of noise Enhances Learning in Neural Networks* In Neural Networks Vol. 5 page 626-637
Caudill, M.	(1989) *Neural Networks,* San Francisco CA Miller Freeman Publications
Caudill, M. & Butler, C.	(1990) *Naturally Intelligent Systems,* Cambridge MA MIT Press
Chakraborty, Kanad	(1992) *Forecasting the Behavior of Multivariate Time Series Using Neural Networks* In Neural Networks Vol. 5 page 960-970
Chen, J.R.	(1990) *Step-size Variation Methods for Accelerating the Back-propagation Algorithm,* IEEE Proc IJCNN Washington Vol. 1 page 601-604

Author	Description
Dawkins, Richard	(1993) *The selfish gene (The biological base of our behavior)*, Oxford University Press Reediting
Dayhoff, Judith	(1990) *Neural Network Architectures: An Introduction,* New York Van Nostrand Reinhold 1990
Dewdney, K. A.	(1985) *Exploring the field of genetic algorithms in a primordial computer sea full of fibs,* Scientific American 253(5) 21-32
Duda, R. & Hart, P.	(1993) *Pattern Classification and Scene Analysis,* John Wiley editor
Eberhart, Russell C. & Dobbins, Roy	(1990) *Neural Network PC Tools* editors London Academic Press
Freeman, James	(1993) *Neural Networks*
Gane, Y. Sarsons	(1982) *Structured Systems Analysis*
Gately, Eduard	(1996) *Neural Networks for financial Forecasting*
Goldberg, D.E.	(1982) *SGA A simple Genetic Algorithm Ann,* Harbor: University of Michigan Department of Civil Engineering
Goldberg, D.E	(1985a) *Optimal Initial population size for binary-coded genetic algorithm,*(TCGA Report Number 86003) University of Alabama The Clearinghouse for Genetic Algorithms

Author	Description
Goldberg, David E.	(1993) Genetic Algorithms in Search, Optimization, and Machine Learning. Reprinted with corrections from Goldberg (1989) Addison Wesley Longman, Inc.
Haykin, S.	(1991) *Adaptable filter Theory*, NJ Prentice Hall
Jastrow, Robert	(1993) *The enchanted loom The human brain and the computer* Edit: Simon and Schuster Reediting
Jonnson, M.	(1988) *The random walk and Beyond*, John Wiley editor New York
Kohonen, Teuvo	(2001*) Self-Organizing Maps,* Springer
Kohonen, T.	(1989) *Self Organization and Associative Memory,* Springer Verlag 3a
Marina, Jose Antonio	(1993) *Theory of Creative Intelligence*, Editor: Anagrama
Miller W. T. & others	(1990) *Neural Networks for Robotics and Control,* Cambridge MA MIT Press
Minsky, Marvin & Papert, Seymour	(1988) *Perceptrons*, Cambridge MA MIT Press Edition Expanded
Monod, Jacques	(1972*) Random and Need*
Moravec, Hans	(1988) *The mechanic man. The future of human and robotic intelligence.*

Author	Description
Simpson, P.	(1990) *Artificial Neural Systems*, New York: Pergamon Press
Trillas, Eric	(1998) *Artificial Intelligence: Men and Machines*
Weiss, Sholom M.	(1991) *Computer Systems that learn*, San Mateo CA Morgan Kaufmann editors

INDEX

3L-BPN, xxi, 40, 43, 45

4L-BPN, xxi, 40, 42, 44-46, 48

Activation, xxi, 15-16, 20-21, 23-24, 31-33, 36, 40, 43-47, 49-50, 53, 55, 68, 72, 95

AI, xxi, 7-8, 90

ANN, xxi, 141

Architecture, xvii, xxii, 19, 27, 49, 52, 64-65, 91, 94-95, 99, 101-102, 106, 118

Artificial, xxi-xxii, 7-8, 15-16, 64, 72, 90, 95, 126, 137, 143

Associative, xxii-xxiii, 56, 58-59, 142

Back, 19, 21, 25-26, 29, 40-41, 48, 56, 61, 67, 140

Biological, xxi-xxii, 15-16, 120-121, 125, 141

BPN, xxi-xxiii, 19-25, 27-30, 35-36, 38, 40, 44, 51-53, 55, 63, 65, 100, 103-104, 106, 108-109, 115, 118-120

Brain, xxi-xxii, 7-12, 14-16, 25, 121, 125, 142

Character, xxii, 9, 58, 75, 78-79, 106

Computer, xxi-xxii, 3, 8-9, 15-16, 57, 66, 68-69, 71-73, 89-90, 96, 125, 141-143

Connection, 14-15, 31, 63-64

Feedback, xxi, 51

Forward, xxi, 25-26, 29-30, 37, 45-46, 49, 51, 53-54, 61-62, 67, 103

Function, xxi-xxii, 8, 14-15, 20-21, 23-25, 31-37, 40, 43-50, 53, 55-56, 61, 65, 95, 103-104

Hidden, xxi-xxii, 20-21, 23, 35-36, 40, 43-47, 49-50, 63, 65-67, 95, 100-101, 118, 121

145

Input, xxi-xxii, 3-4, 12-13, 20-23, 25-26, 30-31, 33-36, 40, 43-44, 46-47, 50-53, 56-61, 63, 65-69, 71-72, 74-76, 78, 80-81, 83, 95-96, 98-100, 102-103, 108-109, 113, 119, 121, 127

Intelligence, xxi, 7-8, 90, 137, 142-143

Layer, xxi-xxiii, 14, 16, 20-26, 30-31, 35-36, 40, 43-48, 50, 52, 56, 58-59, 63, 65-68, 72, 80-82, 95, 98, 100-101, 108-109, 113, 118, 127

Layers, xxi-xxii, 3, 14-15, 20, 40, 43, 45, 49-51, 56, 59, 63, 65, 67, 72, 78, 95, 101, 109, 118, 121

Map, xxiii, 51-52, 78-79

Memory, xxii-xxiii, 11-12, 14-16, 25, 56, 58-59, 64, 68, 103, 142

Net, xxi-xxii, 2-4, 10, 23-27, 29-31, 35-38, 42-49, 51, 53-54, 56-57, 59-61, 65-69, 72, 74, 76, 78, 80-81, 83, 87-96, 98-106, 108-111, 114-115, 117-119, 121, 123, 125

Network, xvii, xxi-xxiii, 2-3, 7-8, 10, 12, 15-16, 19, 21, 25, 27, 29-32, 34, 37-41, 49-52, 54-56, 58-60, 63-69, 72-74, 85, 87-89, 91, 94-106, 110-111, 115, 117-118, 121, 123, 125-126, 137, 141

Neural, xvii, xxi-xxiii, 2, 5, 7-10, 14-17, 19, 25, 30, 38-39, 51, 64-67, 69, 72-74, 76, 85, 87-89, 91, 94-95, 105, 111, 115, 120-121, 123, 125-126, 137, 139-143

Neurons, xxii, 7-8, 12-16, 25, 31, 51, 64-65

Nnet, xxii, 16, 25, 64-65, 81, 87, 91-92, 101-103, 123

N-Net, xxii, 16, 25, 64-65, 81, 87, 91-92, 101-103, 123

OCR, xxii, 9-10, 58, 72

Optical, xxii, 9, 58

Organization, 142

Organizing, 51-52

Parallel, xxii, 49-50, 101, 118

Pattern, xxi-xxiii, 8-10, 20-21, 25-27, 29-30, 35, 37-38, 40, 45-46, 49, 52, 54, 56-60, 62, 65-67, 72, 74-76, 79-82, 95-101, 103-107, 109, 111-114, 119, 121, 125, 141

PHN, xxii, 101

Programmer, xxi, 91, 102

Propagation, xvii, xxi, xxiii 19, 21, 25-26, 29, 37, 40-41, 45-46, 48-49, 51, 53-54, 61-62, 65, 67, 103, 140

Recognition, xxi-xxii, 8-9, 29-30, 56, 58, 101-103, 118, 125, 131

SAM, xxii, 56-57, 59-61

Self, xxii-xxiii, 51-52, 56, 58-59, 142

Software, xxi, 2, 9, 14-16, 65, 87-88, 90, 95, 97

SOPN, xxiii

Training, xxi, 25-26, 30, 32, 38-39, 54, 63, 65, 82, 94, 99-100, 102-104, 106, 108, 113, 119

Weights, xxi-xxiii, 3, 14, 16, 20-31, 34, 36-37, 42-44, 47-50, 52-56, 59-60, 62, 65-67, 95, 99-101, 103-104